THE SHIFT

To Sojourn Grace Collective.

Thank you for teaching me so much about love, community, and wholeness, and for giving me the grace and space to work through many of the ideas in this book.

It's an honor to be your pastor.

Cover design: James Kegley

Print ISBN: 978-1-5064-5549-5

eBook ISBN: 978-1-5064-5550-1

Surviving and Thriving after Moving from
Conservative to Progressive Christianity

THE
SHIFT

COLBY
MARTIN

CONTENTS

INTRODUCTION

IT'S KIND OF LIKE A SURVIVAL GUIDE

One afternoon, while in a photography museum gift shop, I noticed the title of a book so juicy I couldn't not pick it up. *Read This if You Want to Be Instagram Famous*, the bold letters promised, perfectly aligned across the cover of the of-course-it's-square book. Flicking through the glossy pages of pristine people and fabulous food, I skimmed sections covering topics such as choosing the right hashtags, using filters, and everything you'd ever want to know about taking the best selfie (I may or may not have lingered on this section). The final sentence of the introduction promised, "No matter what direction you want to take your feed in, this priceless advice means you can build a following fast, create something to be really proud of and, of course, give up your day job, travel the world and get shit for free."[1]

The book you hold in your hands offers no such promises—unless you believe reduced anxiety, more freedom, and deeper love amount to getting shit for free, because I *will* offer that. Bookstores overflow with how-tos, but this book is not a guide for how to *become a progressive Christian*. There does not exist one single way to be a progressive Christian; therefore the following pages won't tell you what you need to do (or worse, what you need to *believe*) in order to become one.

---

1 Henry Carroll, *Read This if You Want to Be Instagram Famous* (London: Laurence King, 2017), 7.

When I first came up with the idea for this book, and before I had a title worked out, I told people, "It's kind of like a survival guide for becoming a progressive Christian." I balked at outright calling it as such largely because I feared people conflating "survival guide" with "how to." But I noticed people's eyes light up at the term "survival guide," because the movement away from conservative Christianity is no joke. It's hard out there. The path toward progressive Christianity is loaded with obstacles, and surviving is often about the best we can hope for. Yes, I also hope to empower readers to thrive in their new spiritual lives, but I want to be clear from the get-go: this is not a how-to book.

Eventually, I landed on titling this book *The Shift*. This is my attempt to name the process of a person shifting from their conservative Christian communities toward an expression of spirituality that might still connect with some aspects of the Christian tradition but resides within a more progressively minded worldview. In other words, when you move from conservative to progressive Christianity, that's the Shift.

A SURVIVAL GUIDE FOR BECOMING A PROGRESSIVE CHRISTIAN

Terms such as "progressive" and "Christian" are difficult to define—they carry about as many meanings as there are people who use these terms. I trust that you will use, edit, or ditch these labels depending on their utility and value for you.

But so you know where I'm coming from, when I say "progressive," I am referring to someone who affirms and celebrates a diversity of sexual identities and orientations; holds egalitarian views regarding men and women; sees the existence of—and the need to dismantle—

white supremacy; and accepts scientific inquiry as a companion, not a competitor, toward spiritual enlightenment. Progressivism certainly includes more than that, but for me it is *at least* that.

And when I say "Christian," I do so in the broadest sense. My bars for what might render a person Christian are fairly low. For me, the term represents the person who (1) has decided that in Jesus—through his life and his teachings—there exists a trustworthy path for living life to the fullest and they are trying to live in that way, and (2) makes effort to identify with at least some aspects of the religious tradition and heritage that emerged in his name.

Ideally, this book will function like a survival guide. A survival guide is written by someone who has traversed treacherous territory, fallen down its pitfalls, survived its hardships, and then turned around to shout across the ravine, "Yeah, it's no joke out here! But if you'd like, here's what I learned. Perhaps it can make your excursion along similar territory slightly less cumbersome."

In 2014, my wife and I started a progressive Christian church in San Diego called Sojourn Grace Collective. Since then, we've spent untold hours ministering to hundreds of people who have undergone the Shift. Each of their stories carries similar themes of pain, loss, confusion, and loneliness. This book emerges out of both my own experience with the Shift and as a result of shepherding many along the way. The following pages represent my attempts to guide people through the very unique experience of leaving conservative Christianity and attempting to make their way toward some version of faith within a more progressive context. Such a journey tends to leave people lonely, frustrated, confused, and angry (in addition, of course, to the uplifting moments of feeling freer, lighter, and more hopeful than ever). I hope this book normalizes that experience for you, while at the same time offers the occasional helping hand or useful insight as you navigate the obstacles ahead.

A VULNERABLE BOOK

Not to brag, but I'm pretty good at sleeping. Normally, it welcomes me like a freshly hired Walmart greeter. But one evening, just before finishing this book, it treated me more like the Costco exit guard who scans your receipt, glances with unprovoked judgment toward your cart, and won't let you go until you acquire the Sharpie swipe of victory. Frustrated, I stared into the darkness, scanning the receipt of my brain for what held me back from passing to the void. I tossed and turned on my Casper mattress. I fluffed and re-fluffed my Tuft & Needle pillow. *Maybe my issue is that I fall prey to too many Facebook ads? Nah, that's ridiculous,* I thought as I unclasped my MVMT watch.

Finally, after about thirty restless minutes, it hit me: I was anxious about this book. Not in terms of finishing it or meeting deadlines, but the thought of its content becoming public started to make me panic. *That's interesting,* I mused. *This is all stuff you've been preaching at your church for the past six years. Plus, in* UnClobber[2] *you took on one of the most volatile topics in Christianity: homosexuality and the Bible. You're not unaccustomed to entering potentially treacherous territory or questioning dearly held beliefs, so why the anxiety now?* The more I sat with this observation, the clearer it came into focus. It's one thing to preach a sermon to 150 people who know and trust me, and who can engage in immediate feedback and dialogue if needed. But putting the same thoughts on paper for strangers to read, with no potential for dialogue? That's different.

The ideas in this book represent almost an entire 180-degree shift from the belief system I grew up with and practiced for most of my life. The Colby from a dozen years ago wouldn't put his name to even 5 percent of the following observations and insights. Anxiety

---

2 Colby Martin, *UnClobber: Rethinking Our Misuse of the Bible on Homosexuality* (Louisville: Westminster John Knox, 2016).

denied me sleep that night because I knew that once this book releases, there would be no putting the toothpaste back in the tube.

Don't get me wrong, I'm proud of the work I've done and the journey I've traveled. But there's still a vulnerability involved in so publicly recanting on what I used to think, while daring to suggest that I also might have some insight on how to survive (and thrive!) becoming a progressive Christian. Plus, I'm assuming the Colby a dozen years from *now* will likely cringe at parts of this book—because faith (as I'll suggest) implies a dynamic evolving, not a static arriving.

I share this with you simply so that *you* know that *I* know this stuff is vulnerable. Trying to sort through the tangled mess of our spiritual heritages, religious identities, and evolving beliefs can get messy. That's why I sense a survival guide like this might be of some use.

MAKING MAGIC OUT OF MAYHEM

I looped one album as my soundtrack throughout the process of writing this book. The origin story for this album goes something like this: Legendary jazz pianist Keith Jarrett, on the evening of January 24, 1975, showed up at the Cologne Opera after an exhausting five-hour drive through Germany's hillsides to perform for a sold-out crowd. Exhausted and suffering from an ailing back, Jarrett arrived only to discover that his request for a Bösendorfer 290 Imperial concert grand piano had gone unfulfilled, leaving him with nothing but an out-of-tune, rehearsal-grade baby grand whose sustain pedal didn't work. Flustered by the conditions, the American perfectionist announced his intention to cancel the evening's concert and fly home. However, Vera Brandes, the seventeen-year-old German student who organized the entire event, successfully pleaded with Jarrett to stay and play for the more than 1,300 anxious and avid jazz fans.

What transpired that night was nothing short of magic. In a back brace and with an instrument whose lowest and highest keys were unusable, Jarrett improvised his brains out for more than an hour, captivating the breathless audience. If you listen close to the recording, you can actually hear Jarrett moaning at times, while the piano responds with its own groans as he beats every last note out of it. ECM Records recorded the performance and released it later that year as *The Köln Concert*. To date, Jarrett's solo masterpiece has sold more than four million copies, making it the bestselling piano album of all time.

I chose this album as the soundtrack for this book because, to me, Jarrett represents the way many of us feel on this journey toward becoming a progressive Christian: tired, alone, frustrated, and a little beat up. The piano feels a bit like Christianity, that clunky, out-of-tune, partially busted tool we have to work with. It's not perfect, yet we're still drawn to it for reasons we can't always name. The improvised record (which I highly recommend, if that's not obvious) points to the surprising magic that broken people might still make with even the most improbable instruments and in the most unlikely contexts—an apt description of many progressive Christian churches I know. And I'm kind of like Vera Brandes, the one insisting you don't give up. The one in the wings cheering you on, believing in you even when you want to quit and walk away.

I don't think we'll sell four million of these things, but I do think that together, you and I can make a lasting impact for good.

So, to begin, I need to rewind the clock fifteen years to another night when sleep decided I did not merit its company.

11

What Happened to My Faith?

Nothing. You've Still Got It, and It's Working Great

Snoring bounced off every conceivable surface, but that's not why I couldn't sleep.

The clock smirked 2:00 a.m. on the final night of our annual men's retreat, deep in the pine-dusted hills of eastern Oregon. Wide awake, I stared at the cracked ceiling of our log cabin while half a dozen other men—sleeping soundly, but not soundlessly—shook the room with their deep, slightly off-rhythm breathing. My friend Darryl sounded as though he had tried to swallow an Emily Dickinson novel before bed, but it had stuck in his throat, flapping against his windpipe like a two of spades taped to an overeager ten-year-old's bicycle rims. The vinyl mattress—ripped, forest green, barely two inches thick, probably intended for middle schoolers—currently attempting to offer me sleep stood no chance in the battle against such vibrations. Even if I could have silenced the roar of my fellow bunkmates, I stood no chance against the deafening voices inside my own head.

Fifteen years later, I still can't recall what the keynote speaker said during the closing session of our retreat. Likely, he exhorted us to be more biblical manly men—some odd mixture of Braveheart and King David. Still, I'll never forget the flood of thoughts assaulting my consciousness as I lay there, sleeping bag pulled around my ears, desperately not sleeping. Whatever the speaker said somehow unlocked a flurry of seemingly unrelated (yet previously unconsidered) questions inside me.

Why do we think, I surprised myself by asking, *that the mercy of God ceases the moment our earthly lives end? The Bible clearly states that God's love and God's mercy endure forever, yet the church teaches us that these divine attributes are only on tap for, what, seventy to eighty years or so on average? Why do we receive the reliability of God's mercy while oxygen flows through our lungs, but the minute our brainwaves stop, we assume the flow of God's mercy stops with it?*

These thoughts haunted me for hours. I had no idea where they came from, nor what to do with them. I mean, never had I considered the possibility that God might show a person mercy *after* they die. My religious tradition always maintained that our eternal destiny gets locked in on *this* side of death's door. Yet, that night, I couldn't resolve the tension of why the power that raised Christ from the dead should suddenly become powerless at our own deaths. I couldn't understand why my religion limited God's mercy as applicable or efficacious only during a human's lifetime but impotent in the afterlife.

I eventually sunk into a restless slumber, meditating on the words from Lamentations 3 and committing to take them more seriously when I awoke: "The steadfast love of the Lord never ceases;

your mercies never come to an end; they are new every morning." As dawn broke and we packed up to drive home, God's mercies weren't the only thing new that morning.

I'm pretty sure I was too.

DON'T QUESTION THE STATUS QUO

That night, for the first time, I had detected that the clothes of conservative Christianity no longer fit. This discovery left me both exhilarated and terrified. I had worn those clothes my whole life. My alma mater sewed and stitched my cap and gown from those clothes. My uniform as a worship pastor came from the same fabrics. Yet I was entertaining ideas pregnant with the potential to strip me of my wardrobe and exile me from my faith community.

I grew up religiously attending a mixture of Baptist and evangelical churches. As a high school senior, a life-changing experience on the beaches of Southern California led me to abandon my dreams of becoming a graphic designer and instead enroll at a Christian liberal arts college, where I got my degree in pastoral ministry. I felt a strong call to be a pastor, so I dedicated myself to studying the Bible, learning the craft of preaching, and staying firmly planted in the soil of orthodox Christianity. Any attempt to accuse me of heresy was laughable, and my Christian communities loved and rewarded me for it. My strong and outspoken faith inspired others, and they admired my robust knowledge of the Bible. My passion for truth and skill in apologetics were unmatched.

So, why on earth did I entertain the notion that a loving God might opt to extend mercy to a person even *after* they had died? Such suggestions went against everything I had trained for.

After descending the Oregonian mountains, with my snore-filled sleepless night behind me, I met up with my wife and mom for lunch at a Subway in Salem. As we sat and unwrapped our turkey clubs, dodging their excessive oil and vinegar, I recounted my experience from the night before. I shared my musings around God's mercy, and why we suppose it runs out the moment our breathing ceases. It's not that I argued for universalism, as though I suddenly believed that everybody gets to go to heaven when they die regardless of their earthly life. I merely asked what (for me) seemed like interesting questions. Turns out, not everyone at the table found them as interesting. The look of terror in my mom's eyes meant one of two things: either the sandwich artist accidentally put pickles and olives in her footlong, or my fears about how my religious community would receive my questions were on point.

"Colby," she pleaded, setting down her lunch, "the Bible says that Jesus is the Way, the Truth, and the Life. And that no one gets to the Father except through *him*!" Her emphasis on the final pronoun was unmistakable. I nodded along, hearing the concern in her voice and sensing that if I pushed any further, things would go south fast. Her fear that I was toying with untouchables had risen to the surface, confirming my own fear that it wasn't safe to ask questions about deeply cherished beliefs.

If you've ever cast doubt upon traditionally held beliefs, I'm certain you know well what it felt like sitting in Subway that afternoon, lasering my focus on my Sun Chips and hoping the conversation would move on, regretting that I had shared my thoughts at all. You have probably felt that mix of enthusiasm and fear as you're lit up with some new and interesting idea, but also scared to death to talk to your friends and family about it.

When weathering the Shift, most of us discover just how much fear surrounds what ought to be the simple act of asking questions about our beliefs—to say nothing of the sheer terror at the prospect of changing them. Doubt raises all sorts of alarm in the majority of conservative Christian circles. I suggest this fear emerges because we have fundamentally misunderstood the word, idea, and concept of faith.

WHAT HAPPENED TO MY FAITH?

Over the past several years, I've met hundreds of people who have undergone the Shift. When I hear about their journey of either willingly leaving or being forced out of their conservative faith communities, even though the particulars are unique, many of the underlying feelings and experiences show up with amazing regularity. The most common statements reveal concerns around the state of their faith. Frequently, I hear:

I think I've lost my faith.

What happened to my faith?

My faith just isn't what it used to be.

Such responses suggest a few things happening underneath. First, it's obvious that the person in question has recently undergone some sort of transformation. How they feel about their faith now is very different from how they've felt about it in the past. Something (or *many* things) has shifted.

Second, and slightly less obvious, is the presence of anxiety. This could be relatively small, a mild fever of sorts. Or it could range up to a full-blown nervous breakdown, a genuine faith-based freak-out. Regardless, the point is that worry and concern have tagged along during their journey of spiritual transformation.

Finally, statements like these reveal some assumptions around what it means to *have faith*—namely, that faith is a thing we possess and therefore it can be broken, lost, or altered in some way.

Imagine (hypothetically, of course) that I rush into the kitchen, beckoned by a voluminous shattering sound. I scan the room and see our boys, Nerf guns in hand, standing over a turquoise wreckage of ceramic shards. For me to ask "What happened to Mom's elephant?" is a way of saying, "The state of this elephant figurine used to be intact, whole, and complete, but now it is in a new state of brokenness and disarray." When Christians experience the Shift, they ask "What happened to my faith?" because they assumed faith was a possession, a thing to hold on to. Yet now it feels like a shattered tchotchke, blasted across kitchen tile, with this belief over by the sink, that belief landing in the dog's food bowl, and twelve other previously held beliefs lost forever under the fridge and oven.

Next, consider the phrase "I think I've lost my faith." Behind this sentiment is a belief that faith is a quality that can be possessed one moment and lost the next. Recently, I took my sons to a science museum where the main exhibit featured a history of the most innovative advances in video games. Curators transformed the space into massive gaming rooms with consoles and screens everywhere, all free to play and enjoy. One area was contained in a booth, somewhat isolating you from the rest of the crowd, where you could play a game designed to score your singing skills. I stepped in with my youngest son, determined to crush "Love Song" by Sara Bareilles. But the moment I held the mic and went to select the song, I became conscious of all the passersby. My karaoke courage withered; a fear that I'd look silly overwhelmed any excitement I had to see how many notes I could nail. In other words, I lost my nerve. Many people think faith functions just like nerve or confidence—it's a thing we possess that influences us to make certain decisions, and therefore it's also a thing we can lose, thereby changing who we are and what we do.

Even the relatively innocuous statement "My faith just isn't what it used to be" treats faith as a commodity with varying degrees of quality, as though faith is like me and my relationship to jumping. Sure, in high school I could slam a basketball, no problem. But thanks to years, pounds, and entropic calf muscles, my hops aren't what they used to be. In a similar way, it's common for people to reflect on the state of their spiritual selves and feel like they *used* to have a robust, active faith that now feels stale.

To say it again, many people view *faith* primarily as a thing, quality, or commodity that we possess, rendering it susceptible to being altered, lost, or weakened.

That raises the question: If faith is understood as a thing we *have* (spoiler alert, I think it's more than that), then what makes up this thing? In other words, within this commonly held conception, what are the elements or components of faith, and what would lead to it feeling altered, lost, or weakened?

A SET OF BELIEFS

Ask the average religious person what faith means, and they'll probably respond with "Believing in something I cannot see or fully be certain of." Fair enough. Not a bad description. But if you take it another step and ask about *their* faith, now we're talking about something slightly different. The phrase "my faith" is often defined as "the set of my beliefs." In Christianity, this includes what you believe about God, the Bible, sin, Jesus, salvation, the church, the Trinity, and so on.

We tend to bundle all our beliefs into a singular box and wrap it up with a bow labeled "Faith." This collection of beliefs then becomes the thing we possess (a.k.a. our faith), rendering it vulnerable to being altered, lost, etc. I've witnessed over and over that a person will experience a shift in one belief, followed by another and then another, until some Tuesday night in November during a moment of introspection, they take stock of the current things they believe (or no longer believe), and it elicits statements like these: *I think I've lost my faith. What happened to my faith? My faith just isn't what it used to be.*

My high school friend Carlos used to go to church and loved it, and he used to believe that the stories of the flood and Noah, and of the fish and Jonah, were both historical events. He has since reconsidered such stringent beliefs, leaving him feeling like his faith is less than what it used to be. My friend Jessica grew up in the church and used to believe God created the world in six literal days. But now science shows her that's impossible, so she feels like she's lost her faith. And Terry emailed me to share her struggles with believing that God still loves her, cares about her, or even exists, and expressed genuine dismay at what has happened to her faith.

Any of this sound familiar? You used to believe Jesus really did walk on water and magically fed thousands of people, but now you're not so sure. You used to believe the Bible was without error, a perfect book reliable for all of life's answers, but now you know otherwise. You used to believe that only people who accepted Jesus into their hearts would go to heaven when they die, but now you can't stomach such a thought. And when you add up all these shifts in beliefs over the past several years, you genuinely wonder "What happened to my faith?" *and* conclude that maybe, just maybe, you've lost it altogether.

These sinking feelings happen because we have allowed "my faith" to be shorthand for "the list of things I believe." As long as we understand faith to be a thing we possess, a thing made up of a set of beliefs, then we risk feeling like our faith is weakened or lost when our beliefs no longer fit inside the box we've made for them.

A THRIVING FAITH

To begin this process of surviving the move away from conservative Christianity, I want to expand our definition of faith. Many of the struggles and challenges that come up when we shift toward a more progressive expression of Christianity are aided (if not alleviated) by having a more robust view of faith. Yes, there remains a time and place for using "faith" in a credal sense, to communicate that I do in fact possess a certain set of beliefs. We don't need to eliminate that usage altogether. But faith is so much more than that. I hope to equip you with a more empowering, liberating, and beneficial approach to faith.

My wife, Kate, and I host a podcast[1] that engages in topics and questions related to progressive Christianity. One evening while recording, Kate attempted to summarize my position on the topic we were discussing. I felt she didn't quite have it right, so I said that her explanation was a "straw man." Now, I think our producer has since burned the recording of what transpired next, but needless to say, our conversation quickly went off the rails. As it turned out, I had fundamentally misunderstood what the term "straw man argument" meant. I thought it meant your interlocutor had an incorrect or incomplete version of your position, which would make it easier for them to cut it down. However, as I eventually discovered, inherent to the concept of a straw man is that the other person is *intentionally* (or even maliciously) misrepresenting you. While I only intended to say my wife didn't articulate my position well, I used a term that accused her of nefarious motivations. Whether it's the tactic of a straw man or the topic of faith, inadequate definitions can result in not just misunderstandings, but actual harm being done.

Based on my own experience and through countless interactions with Christians experiencing a shift, we do real harm to ourselves as a result of our incomplete and inadequate definition of faith. We end up feeling like we're doing it wrong, or like we're not enough and don't measure up simply because we no longer believe the same things we once did. If we regard our faith as lost or

---

1 Kate Christensen-Martin and Colby Martin, *The Kate and Colby Show*, www.thekateandcolbyshow.com.

broken over our changing beliefs, then it's no surprise that people feel crushed by shame, fear, and inadequacy. And none of these are feelings God wants for you or your life.

We need to redefine how we think about faith. We need to pay attention to those moments when you're at a men's camp, painfully unable to sleep and staring at the spiderwebs in the corner, itchy because the clothes of conservative Christianity no longer fit.

The itchiness is normal. It's okay. It's good. But the accompanying feelings of fear and shame, while understandable, ultimately are unnecessary weights we can discard. Then, with a larger and fresher understanding of faith, and with a lightness in our step, we will get into some of the unique challenges we have faced (or will face) on our journey toward a more progressive expression of Christianity.

In order to survive the Shift, we must retrain our brains to see the modifying or shedding of beliefs not as doomsday signs that our faith is failing, but as beautiful indications that we are witnessing the power of a faith that is thriving.

22

Forsaking the Foundation of Certainty

Letting Go of the Need to Get It Right

As the sun seared the back of my neck, I willed the hands on my watch to speed up. I'd been going back and forth with these two young men—whom I'd only just met—for nearly an hour, arriving at the limits of my conversational patience. The fact that I could place the blame on no one but myself for this predicament intensified my plight.

"How about we meet at the coffee shop across from the church," I had unwisely suggested in an email two weeks prior, "early on Sunday before our service begins?" The two guys sitting opposite me, comfortably shaded under an umbrella, had recently finished my book *UnClobber* and emailed to inquire about meeting up as they drove through San Diego on a road trip. Both identify as gay, and the book initiated their process of integrating their sexualities with their previously held conservative religious convictions. I had caused multiple cracks in the foundation of their belief systems. Most people I hear from attest to how *UnClobber* helped *relieve* their tension, but for my two guests that warm Sunday morning, still green from their very recent Shift, I seemed to have *created* some.

To be fair, these gentlemen did express deep appreciation for how I helped free them to feel like they could be both gay *and* Christian. But once those pleasantries were out of the way and brief introductions were made, I noticed some common themes embedded in their questions as I sipped my Brazilian coffee. A low hum of anxiety flickered at the edges of each query. From their frenetic pace and constant fidgeting, I got the sense that they hoped to sort it all out before the coffee got cold. Though they never put it like this, here's how I would summarize their general posture: *Your book helped us see how we've been wrong in our belief about the sinfulness of homosexuality, which has caused us to question all sorts of other beliefs. We don't know what is true anymore! Please help us decide what to keep from our old religious framework, what to change, and what to abandon.*

As young gay men, they were thrilled to feel unchained from an oppressive reading of the Bible, but not knowing what else might not be true terrified them. In their desperation to find solid ground once again, they turned to me to help them shore up some semblance of "correct" beliefs. They intuited—correctly, in my opinion—that many of their old religious ideas needed to be rethought, if not altogether discarded. However, their fear of complete deconstruction, where they'd be stripped of all the security that religious convictions offer, seduced them to rush to rebuild a replacement dogmatic framework—albeit one atop the exact same foundation. This foundation, I explained, goes by the name of certainty.

Certainty arises as an assurance that we possess the correct beliefs about God, Jesus, the Bible, salvation, and so on. It can provide a firm foundation, a sense of being grounded, and my two new friends' sudden lack of it unnerved them. Their lead anchor exploded out of the mountainside, leaving them desperate for a new handhold to stop their terrifying free fall.

Looking back, I'm sure my casual maneuvering around their pointed questions, my refusal to answer with the clarity and conviction they were no doubt accustomed to hearing from pastors, and my occasional response of "I don't know" did very little to assuage their anxiety. In my defense, I wasn't prepared for a doctrinal inquisition. Not to mention, I tried to retain at least some of my brain power, considering I still needed to preach in forty-five minutes. (You'll be glad to hear I have since reevaluated my policy in taking Sunday morning meetings. I don't.)

My poorly timed coffee with those two young men illustrates a common hurdle one must overcome when undergoing the Shift: our insatiable desire to know the right things and believe them with 100 percent certainty. From spelling bees to SAT scores to racking up piles of money on *Jeopardy*, our culture thrives on getting it right. No doubt, when it comes to performing brain surgery or filing your taxes, rightness is essential. But I lament how this obsession with absolute certainty has crept into religious spaces.

FROM CERTAINTY TO OPENNESS

Somewhere along the way, Christianity became less "Love your neighbor as yourself" and more "Make sure you believe the right things." As I tried to tell my coffee guests that Sunday morning, if you're still convinced the most important thing to God is that you acquiesce to some master list of propositional statements, you're doing it wrong. I'll explore this more in the coming pages, but for now, simply consider that God may not be primarily concerned with what we believe—as counterintuitive as that seems. In order to survive the Shift, we need a different way to think about faith. One that isn't built on certainty, and one that doesn't presume correct belief as the ultimate concern of God. A good starting point is to think of faith more like a verb than a noun.

Conceptualizing faith in this way remains one of the most significant moves I've made in my spiritual and religious life. I now consider faith something I do (verb), more than something I have (noun). As mentioned in the previous chapter, if faith is a noun—something we possess—then it is subject to deterioration and loss. Much of Christianity has thought of faith solely as a noun, where having strong faith means holding the right beliefs with absolutely certainty. But when faith functions as a verb, it becomes something we can practice and embody. While a qualitative aspect still remains (some practices are more effective and beneficial than others), approaching faith as a verb freed me from a lot of the anxiety and fear that permeates a Christianity obsessed with getting it right.

I suggest we conceive of faith like a posture, a way we might hold ourselves in openness and trust. Faith is the conscious decision to say yes to the perpetual possibility of transformation and growth. Throughout the day, my family's cat wanders around our house in search of sunny spots, bright spaces on the couch or the carpet where she might lay to warm her belly. Faith is kind of like that: an awareness that there is a brilliant light shining out there and we are constantly adjusting, shifting, and turning ever so slightly toward it, always staying open not just to the possibility of its presence but also to the idea that the light can change us—and that change is good. And (to risk pushing this metaphor past its usefulness) we understand that even if we find the light on the edge of the couch, there's no sense in planting immovable roots in that spot. We might very well wake up shivering from an afternoon nap having discovered we're no longer in the light. So, once again, we assume the humble posture of openness and trust (i.e., faith) as we continue our quest.

This shift from a hyper-focus on certainty to a posture of openness changed my life. Richard Rohr writes of faith as "a word that points to an initial opening of the heart space or the mind space from our side. Faith is our small but necessary offering to any new change or encounter."[1] In my previous conservative Christian framework, the better your faith, the more impervious to change it was. Now as I think about faith, like Rohr, I see how it dances effortlessly with change. If we can see faith as a posture of openness, then we welcome transformation and growth as friends, not foes. But if we continue connecting faith with certainty, then anything that might promote change becomes a threat. If transformation, growth, and change play the protagonists of our story, then certainty creeps in as the antagonist.

I'm not sure I had much success, but these were the thoughts I tried to share with the two young guys that morning before church. Adopting a particular belief and then locking that sucker down gets many Christians in trouble. We tend to hold our beliefs with a closed fist and correlate the strength of our faith with our ability to resist doubt. Combine this with the incorrect assumption that what God cares about most is that we believe the right things, and you begin to understand why, when you go home for Thanksgiving and tell your family your new thoughts about religion, your Aunt Sally's eyes get big and she starts throwing Bible verses at you. For Aunt Sally, her faith depends on having the right beliefs. Even more, she believes that God's approval of her hinges on whether she holds

---

1 Richard Rohr, *The Naked Now: Learning to See as the Mystics See* (New York: Crossroads, 2009), 116.

her beliefs steadfastly. Your questions about things like historical context or translation issues or "How does that make sense in light of biology and sociology?" therefore become direct threats to her standing with God. Read that last sentence again; it's important. We tend to think of Aunt Sally as closed-minded, but really she's living out her convictions with great integrity. If your core conviction is that God expects you to believe the right things unwaveringly, it makes sense that you would defend them with a ferocious zeal against those who appear as challengers.

Making the crucial shift from faith-as-noun to faith-as-verb would not only liberate Aunt Sally from the chains of certainty, but it would also align her more precisely with how the gospels portray Jesus and faith.

WAS JESUS A GOOD TEACHER?

Imagine a high school teacher who volunteers on Saturdays to help students prepare for their SATs, a test where answers are either right or wrong. The machine reading your test judges you on a single criterion: Did you answer the question correctly? Therefore, the teacher's goal should be to maximize students' odds of selecting the right answer. A good teacher, by this standard, is one who properly instruct students with precise knowledge so they can correctly answer questions. If we use a diagonal line on a graph to measure the caliber of a teacher, we would say better teachers are up and to the right (because they help more students get more right answers), and worse teachers are lower down and to the left (because they fail to prepare students for the test).

Although there's great debate surrounding things like his divinity and messiahship, if asked "Do you think Jesus was a good teacher?," most people say yes. Much of Christianity (especially the conservative variety that we have or are Shifting away from) approaches faith like a cosmic eternal test. The most reductive iterations of Christianity boil down a person's fate to how they answer one question: What do you believe about Jesus? If our eternal state truly depends on having the correct answers to this (or any!) question, then in order for us to call Jesus a good teacher (let alone one of history's greatest) with both a straight face and sincere heart, we should require that he be higher up on that graph alongside the rest of what we call good teachers. In other words, we should expect Jesus to adequately prepare his followers, past and future, to ace the biggest exam of their (after)life.

If what matters most to God is that we believe the right things, then we must conclude that the Jesus of the gospels was in fact not a good teacher. If he had one job to do—prepare students to get the answer right—then he failed miserably.

First, Jesus taught almost exclusively in parables (Matt 13:34), using them intentionally to make it challenging for people to understand (Mark 4:11). Like me stumbling through poetry, the disciples routinely responded to Jesus's parables by asking, "What does it mean?" If the point is right belief, then veiling the answer in riddles doesn't strike me as a good approach.

Second, whether after healing a person or after someone identifies him as the Christ, Jesus frequently commanded people not to say anything. If the most important thing to God (and presumably, then, to Jesus) is that people believe the right things, why go out of your way to shut down the dissemination of truthful information?

Third, Jesus appeared largely unconcerned when people didn't understand him, such as in John 6, when the crowds expressed dismay over his command that they should eat his flesh and drink his blood. He didn't rush to offer any clarification. Can you imagine our good SAT instructor responding to a confused student with, "Oh, well, moving on."? If getting it right is mandatory, and if humanity's eternity depends on correct belief, then how can we call Jesus a good teacher if he didn't do everything humanly (or, hell, *divinely*) possible to teach people the right answers?

Put plainly, if we believe God's primary concern is having the correct beliefs, and if Jesus represents the mission and heartbeat of God, and—to raise the stakes even higher—if the author of Hebrews accurately identified Jesus as the express image of God, then Jesus darn well should have taught people in such a way as to usher them toward their maximum potential for knowing the right answers. If that's not the case, and if the gospels reveal that Jesus did not adequately prepare his followers (to say nothing of you and me two thousand years later) for such a test, then either:

1. we need to stop calling him a good teacher, or

2. we might be wrong about the existence of a divine demand to get beliefs right.

Clearly, my vote goes with #2. The portrayal of Jesus in the gospels does not substantiate a view that God is ultimately concerned with our faith—if by faith we mean believing the right things.

That being said, I believe our relationship with God has everything to do with our *pistis*.

YOUR FAITH HAS SAVED YOU

In the New Testament, the Greek word *pistis* gets translated most often as "faith." Its fullest meaning brings together words such as faith, faithfulness, and trust. In *The Sin of Certainty*, Pete Enns suggests that when we come across *pistis* in many of its 244 occurrences in the New Testament, if we swap out "faith" with "trust," we will get closer to the heart behind the word *pistis*. Translators' insistence on "faith" in virtually every instance of *pistis* has unfortunately reinforced the idea that faith primarily indicates the collection of what we believe. Remembering that *pistis* more precisely means "trust" helps maintain a sense of action and movement when we think about faith in the Bible. Here's what I mean.

Fourteen times in the gospels, Jesus heals/saves (both translate from the same Greek word) a person in response to their *pistis*. For example, Jesus told two different women, "Your faith [*pistis*] has saved you. Go in peace" (Luke 7:50 and 8:49). Removed from context, the phrase "Your faith has saved you" fits nicely within many conservative Christian frameworks, where "faith" (*pistis*) means believing the right things and "saved" (*sozo*) simply means "not going to hell." If that's the case, these stories should reveal women who demonstrated both a possession *and* an expression of correct belief. But that's not what we find. We don't read about women who professed some doctrinal commitment; we read about women acting bold and brazen. Plus, I'd encourage us to consider *sozo*'s other meanings, such as healed, rescued, and made whole. These stories are not about women securing an afterlife mailing address—they are about finding rescue from pain and experiencing wholeness in their being.

In Luke 7, Jesus dined at Simon the Pharisee's home when a woman—a known sinner—crashed the party and boldly anointed Jesus's feet with a combination of tears and expensive oil. This scandalous gesture irked Simon, who couldn't wrap his head around why Jesus permitted such an egregious affront not only to the social order but to religious propriety as well. Jesus applauded the woman's incredible display of love, calling it a beautiful act, and announced the forgiveness of her sins. He closed with, "Your *pistis* has *sozo*'d you. Go in peace."

Then, in chapter 8, a crowd smothered Jesus while a woman, who had exhausted her life savings to find a medical solution for twelve years of nonstop bleeding, snuck up behind Jesus and touched the hem of his clothes. Immediately, her bleeding stopped. Jesus paused to scan the crowd for the person who extracted healing power from him without his knowledge. The brave woman fell before Jesus, explained why she touched him, and testified to her healing. "Daughter," Jesus again proclaimed, "your *pistis* has *sozo*'d you. Go in peace."

If faith is about having correct beliefs, and if it functions as the mechanism by which we experience *sozo*, then I ask you: What belief, what theological concept, what doctrine did these two women possess that prompted Jesus to praise their faith and present them with salvation/healing/rescue/wholeness? According to these two stories, nothing. These stories don't depend on the women's beliefs. Rather, their bold *actions* lead to their life-changing moments. Jesus lauded their bravery and openness, and how they threw themselves humbly at his feet because they trusted that he was good. That he was kind. That he was love. If Jesus was the light shining in the darkness, then they were the kittens sprawling out to warm their shivering bellies. Their faith made them whole not because they expressed correct belief, but because they acted from a place of trust (see how translating *pistis* as trust would be helpful here?).

These two women presented before Jesus not a doctrinal dissertation on the salvific work of the son of God, but (to quote Rohr) a "small but necessary offering to change."

This, I suggest, was the faith that saved them.

APPROPRIATE WINESKINS

The Shift runs deeper than mere cosmetics. You can't simply keep the old house of certainty and slap on a new coat of paint, stage a few ferns on the porch, and replace those outdated windows that annoyingly make your home hotter in the summer and even colder in the winter. Nor is it purely functional. Like Indiana Jones replacing a shiny golden idol with a dirty bag of sand, if we just try to swap out a few old beliefs for some new and improved ones—all the while still prioritizing getting it right—we'll be dodging flaming arrows and outrunning boulders in no time.

The Shift involves a deep, radical transformation. It invites you to see that the essence of your faith grew atop a rotting foundation— the foundation of thinking the point in life is to believe the correct things and do so with certainty. Like sacrificial religious systems that suggest blood sacrifices can appease distant, angry gods, such a foundation needs to die. Only then can a new foundation—built on faith as trust—emerge in its place. And upon that foundation a more flexible, spacious, and life-giving structure—which is to say, your spiritual and religious life—can begin to grow.

Jesus once taught that you can't put new wine in old wineskins (the new wine will burst the old and brittle material)—perhaps one of his clearer teachings. This deep truth resonates with all who undergo the Shift. The new wine consists of convictions such as expanded hearts for all people (especially those on the margins), a sense that our purpose in life must include more than studying for a post-death test, an integration of different scientific disciplines, and leaving behind an angry God who can't stand to be in our presence. The new wine brings life where we once felt flat. It nourishes where it once wounded. It inspires where it used to discourage. Progressive Christians are experiencing, for the first time in a long time (and for some, ever), incredible fruit in their lives as a result of feasting upon this new wine.

But it does not—it cannot—belong inside the old wineskin of certainty and correct belief.

May the new wineskin be stitched with a deeper understanding of what it means to have and to practice faith. May we see faith as a posture of trust, as a journey of transformation, and as a chasing of the light.

Because that, indeed, is a faith that can save you.

3

Six Tools for Survival

Packing for the Wilderness of Progressive Christianity

Lest my story about the Oregonian mountains from Chapter 1 confuse you, I am not what you might call an "outdoorsy type"—unless golf counts; then call me Bear Grylls. So, when I lay out in this chapter six essential tools to navigate the wilderness of progressive Christianity, and as I use the metaphor of tools for surviving the *actual* wilderness, you hereby have my permission to call me a poser. About the only outdoor survival I have done involves figuring out how long I can keep the car running (while it charges my laptop and powers the fan that cools my tent) until it won't start the next day.

Sure, the first cannon blast in the Hunger Games arena would likely be followed by my face projected in the sky (can you starve to death after just five minutes out in the wild?). But as my friend likes to say, I have other gifts. One of those gifts is my keen Google search skills, which is how I curated the following list of the six most important tools to have when it comes to surviving the great outdoors: good shoes, proper shelter, first aid supplies, food and water, a compass, and a flashlight.

In the last chapter, I proposed that we've been lugging around unnecessary items on our spiritual journey, namely certainty and correct belief. We've been told that we need to get the answers right (because this matters most to God) and then lock it down, resisting questions or transformation. However, I've found certainty and correct belief hardly register when it comes to living the abundant life found in the way of Jesus. It's like me towing around my laptop or an electric fan for my tent: not only do they not assist me in surviving the journey ahead, but they actually make it harder.

As with Googling essential tools for surviving the wilderness, I also collected stories from those who've Shifted to help me determine the six most important tools for moving toward a more progressive expression of Christianity. They are trust, openness, kindness, mercy, love, and the Christ pattern of death and resurrection. Like braving the elements, these spiritual tools help us know where we're going, stay on track, sustain us for the journey, shelter us from obstacles, and keep us stable in the uncharted territory ahead. You won't need to visit REI or fork over loads of cash, because these tools come free of charge and are available to you right now.

#1: TRUST (A.K.A. SHOES)

Shoes are everything. What we wear—or don't wear—can signal our socioeconomic status (think Louis Vuitton or Yeezys), our vocational situation (think Red Wing boots or Gucci loafers), and what our upcoming plans might be (think Nike trainers or beach flip-flops). They can symbolize our cultural context, such as resistance (gum boots in the mines of apartheid South Africa), fashion (stilettos on the runways in Paris), or religion (removing your shoes before entering a Hindu home). Plus, you can't deny their enormous psychological power—who didn't get a new pair of sneakers as a child and swear you could run faster and jump higher?

More importantly, shoes save lives. Infection and disease enter through our feet when they're unprotected, explaining why adequate footwear tops any list of the most important things to pack when heading out into the wilderness. You need to prepare for the cold, the wet, the rocky, the steep, and the long stretches in between. If you don't have good shoes, you won't get far.

Likewise, a posture of trust offers us the best chance to survive (and thrive!) on our journey toward becoming a progressive Christian. Hence its place at the top of my list.

Trust animates our practice of faith. Marcus Borg, in *Days of Awe and Wonder*, writes about faith as a way of trusting that the Whole—his way of naming that in which we live and move and exist—is benevolent. Trusting, in other words, that God is gracious, nourishing, and supportive of life. The alternative is to believe that either everything is malevolent and out to get you, or indifferent and meaningless. Practicing the posture of trust, however, changes the way you interact with the world around you because deep in your bones, you believe that the fundamental source underneath everything is in favor of your well-being.

As you encounter people who question and reject you, as you experience the dissolving of doctrines you've long held dear, as you attempt to reassemble some semblance of a spiritual or religious life, do not forget to bring with you the tool of trust. Like a good pair of shoes, it can empower you to navigate the toughest terrains.

#2: OPENNESS (A.K.A. SHELTER)

In spite of my aforementioned lack of outdoor inclinations, our family does camp from time to time. Our coldest experience came in the mountains outside San Diego, where my wife observed that our brand-new tent had openable roof flaps.

"How cool would it be to sleep under the stars?" we asked— evidently rhetorically, because our kids' skepticism nudged us not. The sun blazed during the day, so we didn't anticipate the temperature dropping like it did after we retired to the tent that evening. Separated from the stars by nothing but a thin mesh ceiling, the six of us shivered through a sleepless night. You might be wondering, "Why didn't you just get up and zip the roof closed?" All I can say, dear reader, is that the mind does funny things when under stress, such as whisper to you, "Stay here, tucked inside this warm sleeping bag. Do not get up! It's far worse out there!"

The lack of a solid shelter above our heads left us exposed to the elements. So, when I say openness, *the next essential tool*, is like good shelter, I recognize that it sounds counterintuitive.

Without shelter—be it a tent, a tarp, a cave, a rain jacket, or the belly of a Tauntaun—we fall prey to the relentless pulverizing of any and all exterior elements. Kate and I love the TV show *Survivor* (yes, it's still on, and, yes, it's still awesome). When a tribe fails to build its shelter in time before a storm comes or night falls, the misery on their night-vision-camera faces extracts every last ounce of pity from the viewer. Surviving the wild requires adequate shelter.

You would think that, on our journey toward a more progressive expression of Christianity, being closed off would shield us from the shame grenades lobbed by family and friends. That it might silence the deafening critic in our heads who leverages our past failures against us. That it might ensure we're never hurt again from yet one more church community. However, in its own subversive way, openness offers us the best protection from threats, both internal and external.

Most Christians I've interacted with who have either already Shifted or are in it right now can give a dozen reasons why it makes sense for them to close off their hearts and walk away from church, faith, and the spiritual life. I can't blame the critic or the cynic for choosing to board up their religious self and vow never to pass under the steeple of another church. The pain experienced when leaving or getting kicked out of our conservative community is real, and so is the temptation to lock the door behind us.

Yet, closing our hearts will lock that pain on the inside, where cynicism and bitterness can establish residence and thrive in our minds. A closed heart ensures all our pain remains alive and well, capable of striking at any given moment. As Richard Rohr says, if we do not transform our pain, we will transmit it.

On the flip side, when we bravely open ourselves up and choose a posture of acceptance and humble trust, the pain now has an outlet. It can grow bored of cynicism, tired of bitterness, and move on. Staying open—to connection, to intimacy, to community, to love and being loved—keeps our hearts soft. This is why openness is like shelter; just like shelter protects us from the attacks of the elements, so can openness immunize us from the pain caused by shame and fear. It is the antidote to a hardened heart that, like having no shelter, leaves us afraid and cold.

#3: KINDNESS (A.K.A. A FIRST-AID KIT)

In our family, we feel less concerned about surviving the wilderness than we do with surviving the San Diego Zoo. If you've never been, the incomparable hundred-acre park not only exhibits incredible animals from around the world, but it also challenges visitors with undulating concrete hills as you walk from African elephants to Arctic polar bears. Our youngest kids never met an incline they didn't desire to run down, and the zoo provides them in spades. I'm confident we've left more skin on their sidewalks from the knees and palms of our boys than Child Protective Services would deem acceptable. Yet, whenever I take our four boys to the zoo, without fail, I neglect to pack Band-Aids. I stuff our backpacks full of water bottles, cheese crackers, and trail mix, but for some reason I always forget the first-aid kit. Many, many people have left the San Diego Zoo with a story to tell their friends of how they gave Band-Aids to some poor dad who let his kids fall down a hill and had no means of stopping the bleeding.

Whether for bee stings, poison oak, or crashing down a hill, an essential tool for surviving the great outdoors is a solid first-aid kit. With it, you have salve for wounds and bandages for injury. As you'll discover in the chapters to follow (or as you've already discovered via your own Shift), the journey to progressive Christianity is fraught with sharp objects and painful situations. Experience has taught me that kindness is often the best remedy for spiritual wounds. Like a good first-aid kit, kindness eases pain and prevents infection.

Though similar, kindness and niceness are not exactly the same, and the distinction matters. Being nice comes from a place of feeling inadequate. We do nice things for others because we seek their approval. Nice fears rocking the boat. Nice avoids total honesty because it prefers being liked. Kindness, on the other hand, comes from a grounded place of healthy self-love. We extend kindness to others not because we desire reciprocal goodness or validation, but because we genuinely see and care for the other person's humanity. Kindness requires healthy boundaries, whereas nice people often get trampled over.

Your friends and family may not understand your new ideas and values as you move toward progressive Christianity. From a place of fear (remember, they likely remain fixed in a mindset that God cares first and foremost about correct belief) they may criticize you, question you, or even cast you out of the fold. Responding with kindness not only gives you a chance to minimize their painful responses, but it lays the groundwork for more open and honest communication moving forward. When we respond with our own criticisms and frustrations, or react from a defensive place, we pour salt in the wounds and delay possible repair. But kindness can be a powerful tool for making sure the cuts don't go deeper and the poison doesn't spread.

Over the years, I've watched many people in our church exhibit kindness to their friends and family members who question the merits of progressive Christianity or a church like Sojourn. For some, kindness looks like refusing to engage in a spat on social media, where words often do more harm than help. For some, kindness looks like inviting loved ones to a Sunday service so they can witness for themselves the kind of community we are. On the flip side, sometimes kindness means skipping church altogether when loved ones are in town because they know how uncomfortable Mom would feel. And—I'll unpack this more in chapter 10— sometimes the kindest thing you can do is create new boundaries between you and your old friends and family, because the trust has been so broken that forced interactions, conversations, or relationships will only make matters worse.

Before we move on, I also need to point out that in this journey you will need to be ready to show *yourself* immense kindness. Specifically, past versions of yourself. A common cycle among progressive Christians involves reaching new levels of awareness, then looking back in horror at what we used to believe and how we used to treat people. Therefore, make sure you stuff your backpack with plenty of kindness (oh, and maybe a few Band-Aids, in case you visit the zoo the same day I do).

#4: MERCY (A.K.A. FOOD AND WATER)

When my oldest son was six, one night at dinner he asked his mother and me, "How long can you live without water?" Why he had dehydration and mortality on the brain, I'm not sure, but I remember confidently answering, "Probably two to three weeks."

Kate burst out laughing—not at our son's question, as I expected, but at my answer. "Two or three *weeks?* Try two or three *days!*" she said. She went on to suggest that perhaps I was thinking of food? Oh, right. Oops. This is just reason 1,264 why Kate handles the homeschooling.

As I'm sure you know (evidently better than I do), while you can last for some time without food, without water you'll barely last the time it takes to binge two seasons of *Game of Thrones*. Any guide worth trusting will insist you bring plenty of water (and snacks!) if you want to survive the great outdoors.

When denied food and water, our machine of a human body tries to buy time by initiating an automatic series of metabolic modes. Important resources get reallocated to the most vital organs, breaking down less-necessary elements into those most critical for survival. Put simply, when the body doesn't get the food and water it needs, it collapses in on itself and the whole thing grinds to a stop.

Without mercy in our spiritual survival kit, we also slowly cave inward and initiate modes of self-destruction. Jesus once instructed religious teachers to meditate on the prophet Hosea's words that God "desires mercy and not sacrifice." Why not sacrifice? Because the sacrificial system establishes boundaries and builds walls. It divides what is good and what is bad, what is holy and what is profane, what is clean and what is unclean. To engage in sacrifice fundamentally assumes a distant and separate God whom we may draw in only through a mediator. In short, sacrifice inherently excludes God from us, and us from others.

Mercy, however, moves in the opposite direction of sacrifice. It does not erect barriers; it eradicates them. Mercy moves toward the other, obliterating any illusion of categories such as clean and unclean. In short, mercy inherently embraces.

I suggest that mercy is like food and water because it keeps our systems up and running, preventing us from the slow death of isolation. When we insist God exists out there, cold and distant from us—and unable to withstand our presence because we are bad, unclean, or unholy—this deprivation of the Divine causes us to shrivel up and die (not unlike the body starved of food and water).

Exclusion keeps us apart, whereas embrace pulls us together. So, pack a healthy dose of mercy for the road—your well-being depends on it.

#5: LOVE (A.K.A. A COMPASS)

As Bill Nye taught me in fifth grade, Earth is a large magnet pulling one force north and an opposite force south. Lay a needle across a cork, place it in water, and you'll see it swivel to align with Earth's north and south poles. Voilà, a compass—a must-have tool for survival. As long as you have one, you can find true north and navigate from there.

For the conservative faith communities we came from, "correct belief" is the goal. It shines as their north star. Therefore, you could argue that whatever mechanism they use to point them north functions as their compass. Insert the Bible. Many church or religious organization websites have a designated page to display their statement of beliefs. There, nestled between parentheses, they list verse after verse as their defense for whatever particular point of belief they deemed essential enough to publicly proclaim. If their north star (a.k.a. the goal of the whole matter) is correct belief, then the Bible serves as their compass, ensuring they're on the right path.

As you construct a more progressive expression of your Christian faith, I propose you decide now that love—not religion, not holy books, not tradition—will be your compass. If you do not know what direction to go in any given situation, you could do much worse than to simply follow love.

Imagine the following description on the back of a compass's packaging:

> The miraculous compass inside this box never fails! It will always protect you, and as long as you have it, no matter how dire your situation may be, you can have hope that things will get better! This compass does not seek its own well-being, but only the best interest of you, the owner. Should you stray, fear not; it will lead you back again and keep no record of your failure. This compass is patient and kind, so even if you've never used one before, you can trust it to always be there for you.

That would be a mighty fine compass indeed. You might've noticed that in this imaginary miracle compass description, I borrowed from Paul's words in 1 Corinthians 13 as he described why love reigns as the greatest force in the universe. That's why I use it as my compass, trusting it will never fail me and will always point me in the direction I need to go.

But love is a tricky thing, isn't it? It sounds warm and flowery to say, "Use love as your compass. It will never fail you!" What does that even mean? Meditation guru Sharon Salzberg describes love not so much as a feeling but more as an ability. Meaning, inside we all carry the capacity to give and show love, with or without the feels we commonly attach to the concept. And according to M. Scott Peck, love is "the will to extend one's self for the purpose of nurturing one's own or another's spiritual growth."[1] I invite people

---

1 Quoted in bell hooks, *All About Love* (New York: William Morrow, 2000), 4.

to use love to direct them through life because we all have the *ability* and the *freedom* to choose actions that can nurture the well-being of yourself and those around you.

Rules, regulations, religion—these can act as obstacles to a person's flourishing. But when love is our compass, like Jesus transcending the limitations of the religious customs that shackled many of his peers, we can break through and better see what paths might move us or those around us forward in spiritual growth.

#6: THE CHRIST PATTERN (A.K.A. A FLASHLIGHT)

The pre-chorus of Semisonic's "Closing Time"[2] nicely articulates what I call the Christ pattern: "Every new beginning comes from some other beginning's end." First the dying, then the rising. Of course, we see this pattern in Jesus's death and resurrection, but the same pattern plays out again and again in our lives: the old must pass away so that the new can come. Darkness falls when the sun sets, yet it cannot hold at bay the piercing light of the eventual and inevitable rising. This is the way of things—death followed by resurrection.

When it's pitch dark outside, miles away from the manufactured glow of electricity, a flashlight ensures you know where you're going. Should you approach an obstacle such as the edge of a cliff, a pit of quicksand, or a narcoleptic opossum, the light from the magic stick in your hand prevents you from certain doom. The Christ pattern secures the final spot on the essential tool list because, like a flashlight, it illuminates both the direction we ought to go and the paths we should avoid.

For example, when my wife and I are in conflict, I choose withdrawal, retreat, and shutting down as my go-to modes of self-

---

2 Semisonic, "Closing Time," *Feeling Strangely Fine*, MCA, 1998.

preservation. These well-trodden paths are comfortable to me. Even if I were stumbling around in the dark, I could traverse them by memory. They call to me as the paths of least resistance. They entice me with offers of freedom from pain. All lies, of course, but years of traveling that road conditioned perfect Colby-sized ruts that make it oh so tempting. However, when I'm mindful, when I can take a breath and notice what is happening inside of me (namely, shutting down and retreating), I can find the necessary space to call to mind the Christ pattern of death and resurrection. This knowledge empowers me to choose the harder, scarier path of engagement and connection. It feels very much like a death to the self I've spent thirty years constructing, but it realistically provides the only way forward if what I want is a meaningful and honest relationship with Kate. This tool, the awareness of the Christ pattern of death and resurrection, maps out for me what paths lead to life and what paths lead to destruction.

I've encountered hundreds of people who've testified that something in their life needed to die as they moved away from conservative Christianity. Specific beliefs that held them back or trapped them in shame needed to die. Spiritual practices such as prayer, Bible study, and corporate worship often needed to end (or at least temporarily pause). Relationships or connections with communities might have demanded dissolution in order for them to find a healthier and happier future. These (often difficult) choices all felt like a dying of sorts, yet thanks to the Christ pattern, their stories always had a way to birth new life out of the graveyard of what they lost along the way.

NOW WE'RE READY

For the remainder of this book, I'll describe many common obstacles Jesus followers face while making the Shift to become a progressive Christian. Sure, the dangers aren't starvation, infection, or death by harsh elements, but ask those who've endured the Shift and they will tell you that the wounds inflicted on the spiritual journey are no less painful.

I firmly believe that as long as we carry these six tools, no obstacles will prove too hard. Jesus famously said, "Whoever wants to find their life must first lose it." That simple (but not easy) instruction says it all. We can *trust* that if we stay *open*, responding to injuries with *kindness* and *mercy*, and choosing the path of *love* as we continue down the scary, vulnerable, hard, and narrow way that leads to certain *death*, then we will surely discover a flourishing, abundant, *resurrected* new life on the other side.

4

Talking, Thinking, and Feeling about God

What to Do When the Idea of God Stops Making Sense

God. A word that both names the subject of this chapter and works as a sort of sigh. An utterance of awe, marvel, and overwhelmedness. Because, honestly, where does one start when trying to think about the creator of everything? *God.*

Let's start by expunging expectations that this chapter will answer all your God-related questions. I doubt you actually thought it would, but perhaps subconsciously you harbor a desperate hope for at least *some* answers. That makes sense, considering the nature of this book. But, sorry, I don't have them. Thankfully, though, surviving the journey of becoming a progressive Christian doesn't hinge on getting the answers right. Trust me when I say you don't need a new airtight theology of God in order to live a whole and flourishing life. The abundant life Jesus spoke of does not require us to know, for instance, whether God can create a rock so large that God cannot lift it (nor whether we believe God foreknew or even predestined that I would use such a cliché example). As mentioned in chapter 2, we must avoid the temptation to merely replace our old beliefs with new ones if we haven't yet dislodged ourselves from a foundation built upon certainty. So, yes, this chapter will address a few obstacles when it comes to the topic of God. But we won't satisfy ourselves by merely upgrading our old ideas about the almighty for newer, sexier, more expansive ones—even if part of the Shift does involve such leveling up.

Moving away from conservative Christianity opens up new ways to think about, talk about, and feel about God. I don't mean simply trading in red apples for green ones because red apples are gross, and if we just get the right apples then all will be well. No, it's more like we're leaving apples behind altogether and discovering a world full of bananas or lampshades or hand soap. (Sorry, did you expect airtight metaphors while trying to talk about God?)

The following pages won't present a comprehensive explanation of the *right* ideas about the creator of the cosmos—as though that could even be done. I offer no outline to organize a reconstructed view of who or what or why (or even if) God is. And even if I wanted to try, there's no such thing as a "progressive Christian way" to think about God anyway. Good gravy, if you thought there were diverse opinions of theology within your old conservative communities, then buckle up for the Wild West of progressive Christianity. It's a smorgasbord of spirituality and suppositions out here—which can drive a person mad if they're convinced the game is still about apples.

Before you read further, I wonder if you would indulge me. Take a deep, slow breath, and imagine yourself relaxing just a bit.

Imagine what it might feel like to be unburdened from the idea that you must know the truth about God. Imagine having a lightness inside you, a playful posture toward questions about the alpha and omega, with curiosity replacing any anxiety. Imagine God as a parent, overjoyed by young children strewn across the living room rug, playfully testing out their limitations and curious of how their parent will react. If God's nature at all resembles that of a human parent's, then God will surely respond with pure delight, unbothered by the reality that not only do the children not know everything there is to know about their parent, but most of their ideas are preposterously wrong. And it matters not one bit.

Did I care when one of my boys once thought I was two feet tall and eighty-four years old? Did it offend me when one of my boys screamed through tears, insisting I didn't love him because I wouldn't let him have a third cookie? Did I respond in anger when my toddler sons didn't understand what I did for a living or why I left the house every morning? Of course not. And if even I, a flawed and bumbling father, can hold such space for my children's ignorance—while simultaneously delighting in nothing but their very being—how much more might the one who gave birth to us all?

GOD AND GENDER

Speaking of God giving birth to us all, we need to talk about how we talk about God. Historically, Christianity has talked as though God is male, and this is a problem.

You may have already noticed that when I refer to God, unless I'm making a very specific point about a masculine or feminine attribute of God, I don't use pronouns. This is primarily because, simply put, God has no body or biological form; therefore using pronouns such as *he* or *she* strikes me as both inaccurate and misleading. I work hard to be precise in my speech because God truly is not a he, and it makes little sense to say otherwise. But beyond mere technicalities, I've refused to refer to God as he/him ever since I was awakened to the many harms done as a result of coupling our ideas of God to maleness.

Ancient cosmology took for granted that the gods had gender identities. Many, if not all, writers of the Bible assumed God (Yahweh in the Old Testament and Heavenly Father in the New Testament) was in fact a male divine being. Their ignorance—well intentioned though it might have been—created a Jewish, and later Christian, culture founded on stories wherein the nature of God and the male gender were synonymous. God as a *he* litters the pages of our holy books. As a result, we've inherited the tragic side effect that women are seen as less than. It shouldn't take more than a moment of reflection to see that if we think of God as male, then our minds will associate all things male with godliness. Conversely, if you move across the spectrum toward femininity, you move away from godliness. As I said, this is a problem.

Modern humans have the advantage of rejecting outright the ancient three-tiered view of the cosmos. We know no gods live beyond the stars. We know the creator has no body. We know God is not a man. But try telling our collective subconscious that! We've been steeped in it for so long that even though we know intellectually that God does not have a penis, we can't stop saying *he* and *him*. My wife calls this the water we swim in, and the water is not innocuous. Its toxicity diseases everything it touches, leaving even those who climb out of the mire ill with inborn ideas about the superiority of men. Hence my efforts to stop calling God *he* or *him*, a necessary step to scrape off the residue of the pond of patriarchal language.

In my experience, many conservative Christians see no issue with the water. Even though they also know it makes no logical sense, they continue referring to God as male. Perhaps they can't change because too much is on the line: biblical inerrancy (after all, the Bible is filled with God-as-male language . . . however, this conveniently ignores when the Bible refers to God using feminine language); complementarian theology (which ensures that men remain the head and women stay in subjugation . . . I mean *service*) and beloved old hymns that just wouldn't be as much fun to sing anymore ("Thi-i-s is my divine parent's world" just doesn't have the same ring).

While it occasionally makes for clunky writing, and adjusting my verbal lexicon has taken time to feel natural, not using pronouns for God has been a commitment of mine since 2012. I realize it sounds weird to anniversarize when I stopped referring to God as *he,* but I share that because it illustrates the process of journeying toward a more progressive expression of Christianity. Your entire paradigm doesn't collapse all at once. It's a series of falling dominoes, and the sequence of which domino knocks down which belief in what order varies from person to person.

By time 2012 rolled around and I finally realized I could no longer in good conscience refer to God as *he,* I was already a solid three years past the point at which the Evangelical Sorting Hat would've placed me in House Servetus, the home of heretics and false prophets.[1] Plus, a full year had already passed since my former evangelical megachurch fired me on account of my LGBTQ-affirming theology. In other words, it took several years of traveling down the path of progressive Christianity before the domino of "God as male"

---

1   Famous heretic Michael Servetus was a Spanish theologian and scientist in the sixteenth century whose nontraditional view on the Trinity, combined with his opposition to infant baptism, landed him on reformer John Calvin's naughty list. For his "crimes," Servetus burned at the stake on October 27, 1553. I'm not saying I necessarily agree with Servetus's views, but his name was too deliciously similar sounding to Severus Snape, a notorious Slytherin, that I had to use it. Fun fact: the real Sorting Hat at pottermore.com indeed placed me in House Slytherin. Makes sense.

toppled. I spent a good chunk of time solidly progressive *and* still calling God *he* and *him* before I confronted how the sole usage of male pronouns for God perpetuates misogynistic views and behaviors.

Looking back, I see how de-gendering God forced a reckoning of my own internal misogyny. Because my religion always presented God as male, I lived my entire life all-in on the idea that masculine attributes were superior to feminine ones. Sure, most of my misogyny simmered at the subconscious level, but the deeper a thing gets buried, the more it can rot, fester, and turn the surface sour without you even realizing. I, like so many in our churches (and even those outside it, because we live in a Judeo-Christian culture), walked around believing men are superior to women.

My gut tells me that my slowness to drop male pronouns for God was less driven by theology (as I've said, *Come on, people. We all know God is not a man!*) and more by a resistance to face my own prejudices against women and femininity. Honestly, I am still weeding out those poisons, which is why I call myself an aspiring feminist. I believe one massive step in the right direction involves changing how I think and talk about God regarding gender.

Even if good-hearted people want to argue around it, they can't deny the math: if God is male, or even if all we use are male pronouns for God, then being a man is more godlike than being a woman. That means man > woman. And that lie creeps out from the depths of hell and must be abolished. This explains why, as you move away from a more conservative view of Christianity, you will notice how many progressive Christians either don't use pronouns at all for God, or bounce back and forth between *he* and *she* as a way to re-gender the full expression of the God who created humanity "in God's own image, in the divine image God created them, male and female God created them" (Gen 1:27).

If that doesn't describe you yet, and you still primarily use male pronouns for God, I hope you'll spend time considering the inevitable side effects on you and those around you. For both men and women, connecting God with maleness impacts us whether we're conscious of it or not.

GOD AND BEING

What do training wheels, contraceptives, and ice in your bourbon have in common? They each provide a helpful service that, down the road, could function as a hinderance. Eventually, you learn to balance a bike, you might decide you want children after all, and you recognize the superiority of drinking your whiskey neat.

Similarly, thinking of God as a being—which is to say, as an object out there somewhere who occasionally fiddles with events here on Earth—can be a helpful concept, until it isn't. Though they may not have words to articulate it (indeed, as you're about to witness, I barely do either), Christians on the path toward a more progressive faith eventually butt up against discontent with how they think about God. It might start as small as "Is God *really* in control of everything?" and grow to "Does God even *exist?*"

I cannot overemphasize how normal these thoughts are. How we picture God in our minds, who or what we believe listens on the other line when we pray—all of that gradually developed as we grew up and formed the basic structure of our beliefs, which functions as a skeleton upon which to hang everything else. While safe and cozy in our conservative communities, we rarely had reason to question this structure. We took for granted that of course God exists, of course God is a being out there who sees and hears us, and of course God interacts with history here on Earth (though to what degree, we likely never could fully articulate).

Now that the clothes of conservative Christianity no longer fit, however, we will surely find ourselves exposed to the crisp, frigid air of doubt and skepticism biting at our naked bones. Thoughts of an atheistic insurrection will rise to the surface, surprising us by their feral tenacity and mocking us for having never considered their arguments before. Our previous naïveté about ourselves, God, and the world around us slow our spiritual life to a halt, lulling us to an agnostic slumber. We're tempted to throw in the towel of theism when we assume our options are either the God of Michelangelo's Sistine Chapel paintings or nothing at all.

But pit stops of varying conceptions of the divine exist between the coastlines of a *700 Club*–style God who grants Learjets to toothy preachers, and the Dawkinsian delusion of god. You need not give up on the idea of belief in God merely because the version handed to you in the past no longer makes sense. Leave behind anything resembling an old white man in the sky, yes. But do not despair thinking that atheism must be your new home.

If you grew up in a Protestant or evangelical tradition, you probably learned to think of God as a sort of super being—very much like you and me, but cranked to eleven. We are wise, but God is wiser. We are strong, but God is stronger. And so on. Most importantly, to think of God as a super being requires God to be an object, a being separate from and superior to us. This being is all knowing, all powerful, and lives or resides in heaven.

At some point along the way, humanity realized the Earth is not flat, there is no heavenly firmament above where some gods reside, nor is there a place under the Earth that houses death and other gods. It's hard to know which of the Biblical writers knew this and which wrote firmly from inside a three-tiered cosmology. Some writers, while speaking of "God above," surely employed such language metaphorically (while others likely meant it literally). Regardless, once the Scientific Revolution hit, all people knew there was no God above, so we made the subtle shift to speak of God as "out there." Still, the language implied God was a being, an object separate from creation, who existed somewhere . . . just really, really far away. Occasionally, this God "out there" would visit Earth or manifest in some way, most notably as the clothed-in-human-skin Jesus.

It is precisely this way of thinking about God—as an object, a being, separate from us—that eventually comes under scrutiny for many people on their journeys toward progressive Christianity. And rightly so, for God as a super being is problematic from a scientific, moral, and biblical viewpoint.[2] These problems explain why some have needed to drop the word God altogether. Not as a declaration of disbelief in God, but because the word God is so intertwined with assumptions and expectations of a being up/out there that it requires too much mental gymnastics to say the word and think or feel something different.

Some progressive Christians have rediscovered the mystics within Christian tradition, who used terms such as *Mystery* and *Divine* to name the reality of God. These words help us conceptualize how God cannot be contained by language and does not exist as a separate being out there. For the mystic, if we can know it, see it, taste it, or touch it, then it obviously cannot be God because God is deeper, higher, and beyond. I'm reminded of the Psalmist who wrote, "Where could I go to get away from your spirit? Where could I go to escape your presence? If I went up to heaven, you would be there. If I went down to the grave, you would be there too!" (Ps 139:7–8). This is not a God who is like us but greater; rather, it is a God who transcends *being* itself. Or, you might say, all that *is* is contained and held within God.

Another way to think of God comes from twentieth-century

---

2 For more on this, I highly recommend *Honest to God* by John Robinson. It's the best and most accessible resource I've found for understanding the move away from God as a super being.

theologian Paul Tillich, who said God is the ground of being. In this way, God precedes both subject and object and exists as that by which the possibility of a relationship between subject and object might even spring forth. When I say "I love my wife," I am the subject and she is the object (of my love). For Tillich (and many progressive Christians I know), God does not exist in this way, as an object we might love. Rather, when relational connectivity happens in the world, it happens as a result of God. You might use words such as *Source* or *Energy* to talk about God in terms of the ground of being. Think of the apostle Paul's words to the people in Athens: "For in him we live and move and have our being" (Acts 17:28 NIV). Everything that exists is *of* God and *in* God. God is neither the flower in bloom nor the gardener with her watering can, but the soil from which everything grows. (Except not, because in that metaphor the soil is yet another object, so technically it couldn't represent God. Fun, isn't it?)

You could also think of God as *Event*, which, bizarre though it may sound, best describes how I most often conceptualize God. To think of God as *Event* is to speak of that which calls us, summons us, and invites us forth. Thought of this way, God doesn't exist; God *insists*.[3] Now, I admit that the first three years after hearing that phrase, I thought it was rubbish. God doesn't "exist"; God "insists"? *Pfff, okay*. Then, one day it just made sense to me, perhaps because I had spent long enough marinating on the possibility that God is not a separate object, a being to whom one can relate in a subject/object manner. Once that idea had dislodged from my initial conscious reaction when I thought of God, I began to grasp how God might be like an *insist*-ing force that calls people in to action.

One of my favorite verses in the Bible is 1 John 4:8, which

---

3 John D. Caputo, *Hoping Against Hope: Confessions of a Postmodern Pilgrim* (Minneapolis: Fortress Press, 2015), 114

simply declares that God is love. Love, like God, is not an object. It makes sense when I say that love compels me to do the dishes when I get home from work. Love is the force that directs me to read a book with my son at night instead of playing *Clash Royale* on my phone. My commitment to a posture of love within relationships means I don't shut down when I get upset, but I show up and communicate honestly. Love beckons, invites, and inspires. Love calls us to fight for the marginalized, march for the oppressed, and seek the liberation of those on the underside of empire. To see God as Event is similar. God isn't in the sky saying, "Go love your neighbor." Rather, when I go love my neighbor, that is me responding to the summons and the reality of God. God does not exist in the sense that God is an object, separate from you and me. God is that which insists humanity show up for justice and mercy. When we respond to violence with compassion, that is God. When we choose forgiveness over revenge, that is God. To speak of God as Event is to say that God is what happens when grace emerges.

It has been incredibly helpful for me to have language for how to think about God in those moments when the idea of God as a being up/out there no longer makes sense. Should you find yourself in similar points of tension on your journey toward becoming a progressive Christian, may God as Mystery or Ground of Being or Source or Event become viable ways for you to maintain and strengthen your connection with God.

If this section only further confused you, you're not alone. Even as I wrote it, I had to acknowledge that I'm merely beginning to grasp other ways of conceptualizing God beyond that of a being up/out there. Perhaps you'll make a mental note of this section and return to it another day. There might come a time when suddenly the idea of God no longer makes sense to you. Like a thief in the night, it'll be unexpected and unsettling. When that happens, try rereading this section. Perhaps certain furniture in your mind will have shifted, opening up spaces within your consciousness for these ideas to land in a new way.

GOD AND YOU

In *The Lego Movie*, the character Bad Cop/Good Cop reminds me of how I used to feel about God. Which God do I get today: the nice one who loves me and delights in my well-being, or the scary one who's raging mad because I lusted during that Carl's Jr. commercial?

The world many of us came out of teaches this sort of dual-natured God, a confusing combination of loving and merciful, yet wrathful and just. ("Just" in this context always meant "dispensing punishment to wickedness," as though the highest form of justice resembles retaliation and consequences. Progressive Christianity gifts us with the renewal of the biblical vision of restorative justice, which maintains that true justice looks like renewal and restoration, not doling out death sentences to evildoers.) With a straight face— and I know, because I must've delivered the line a hundred times— pastors and theologians pontificate that God holds these two (clearly mutually exclusive) postures at the same time. One imagines God jamming to Gnash's 2017 hit as Olivia O'Brien belts the hook, "I hate u, I love u, I hate that I love u."

Which is it? Does God hate us or love us? Many of us were sold the lie that the answer is yes.

Further, our spiritual leaders told us we should feel grateful that a wrathful and just God would stoop to love such loveless and sinful creatures as we. It left us feeling like the eroded partner in an abusive relationship, listless and stripped of our humanity by the anger of our more perfect lover, yet somehow feeling lucky because at least they "love" us—and after all, do we even *deserve* to be happy?

If at any point upon leaving conservative Christianity you found yourself unsure of how to feel about God (thanks to the aforementioned cluster of messages about how God feels about *you*), then you are completely normal. It makes sense to be confused, calloused, or cynical by the whole thing. The Bad Cop/Good Cop God is crazy-making, which is why one of the deepest gifts of progressive Christianity has been its unrelenting insistence regarding the illusion of Bad Cop. There is no angry, wrathful, bloodthirsty God, so holy and pure that the very idea of your presence screams abomination.

Dear reader, God's essence consists entirely and purely of love. Taking anthropomorphic liberties—which is to say, for the moment, I'll personify the divine with humanlike characteristics—God's default posture toward you is only and always love. Of that I have no doubt. This belief sits at the top of my short list of things I would stake my life on. Yes, I've let go of certainty on myriad beliefs, but that God contains only unconditional love for you I do not waver. And this divine love comes free of charge, of course. No magic prayers required. No specific beliefs expected. It is the living water that cannot be packaged or sold or manipulated, and it is without contamination. There are no buts to this love. No "God loves you, but . . ."

If we must speak of wrath, let us trust it is like God in Eden saying to Adam and Eve, "Who told you you were naked?" The divine claws come out when God's children are led to believe they are anything other than inherently beautiful and worthy of love. Yet even then, the swipes of the Almighty's adamantium[4] aim only at fear and shame, never at Phil or Shauna. And should Phil or Shauna ever become conduits for passing fear and shame onto others, God's heart would break at how Phil and Shauna—beloved children they also are—once must've had their own hearts broken first. You see, behind

---

4 Adamantium is the fictitious supermetal from the world of X-Men out of which the character Wolverine's claws are made.

any act of evil are merely layers and layers of shame, ignorance, and pain. Which is why love's ultimate response is always compassion, mercy, and grace. Not punishment, not damnation—those are the responses of one who is afraid, and perfect love casts out fear.

If you hear only one message from this chapter, hear this: you are free. The cage of confusion that God somehow both loves and hates you, which has imprisoned you for far too long, is not locked. You do not have to stay in it; indeed, you must not. Step through the door, breathe in the air of freedom, and receive the gift of knowing how much God delights in you.

How should you feel about God? Well, imagine how you might feel toward someone who believes in you completely, will never leave your side, wants only the best for you, and cheers you on toward becoming the best possible version of you. Yeah, that feels pretty good, doesn't it? Go ahead and feel *that*.

Returning to 1 John 4:8, "God is love," I'll leave you with with my adaptation of the famous love passage in 1 Corinthians 13:4–8. Feel free to put this on your bathroom mirror—either the whole thing or just the line that shimmers brightest—as you work to retrain your brain on how to think and feel about God.

God is patient.
God is kind.
God does not envy, nor boast.
God is not proud.
God does not dishonor others.
God is not self-seeking, nor easily angered.
God keeps no record of wrongs.
God does not delight in evil but rejoices with the truth.
God always protects, always trusts, always hopes,
    always perseveres.
God never fails.
Amen.

5

Believe (in?) Jesus

What to Do with the Question "Who Is Jesus?"

Had I been one of Jesus's twelve disciples, I guarantee I would've panicked that afternoon just outside Caesarea Philippi when he turned his questions toward us: "What about you guys, who do you say that I am?"

We've just told him what we've heard around town, about how other people think of him: "Some say John the Baptist, or Elijah, or one of the prophets. More or less, the general consensus is that you're a dead prophet who's come back to life. Hilarious, right?" We chuckle, unsure if that might *actually* be the case. But now he's asking what *we* think about him. Crap.

We've been following this guy for over a year, and if there's one thing we've learned, it's that we almost never get his questions right.

This one, about his very identity, feels particularly weighty . . . and personal. Would messing this one up get us kicked out of the group? Most of us already ditched the family business in order to walk dusty roads, pester pharisees, and subvert the Empire with him.

Perpetually unafraid to stick his dirty, open-toe-sandaled foot in his mouth, Peter pipes up, "You are the Christ." A couple of us wince, catching each other's anxious eyes as we peek to see how Jesus responds.

He doesn't. At least, not at first. He doesn't even turn around. Typical. Did he hear Peter? We can't tell. He exhales loud and slow, and looks off into the distance, as he often does. We wait, hoping Peter answered correctly. After all, we've sort of been banking on Jesus being the long-awaited Messiah. Finally, he speaks.

"Don't tell anyone," he says.

WHAT DO YOU THINK ABOUT JESUS?

To state the obvious, Jesus stands at the center of Christianity. A person's connection to and engagement with the Christian religion emerges out of their beliefs and ideas about Jesus. The question Jesus asked his disciples in Mark 8:29, "Who do you say that I am?," is the same question men and women respond to today when they decide to follow in his Way.

In most conservative circles, answers to this question flow easily:

"You are the son of God."

"You are the savior of the world."

"You are God in the flesh who died for our sins and rose again so that we might have eternal life."

One obstacle on the journey toward becoming a progressive Christian, however, involves a disruption in our ease of answering "What do you think about Jesus?" We might still say we love Jesus and that we follow and believe in him. But now the particulars of those beliefs feel less secure. Do we still believe he is the Christ? The savior of the world? God in the flesh? That he was born of a virgin, lived a sinless life, died on a cross, and bodily rose from the dead?

Of all the obstacles addressed, this one feels the scariest for many people. We've spent our lives anchored to the idea that being a Christian means possessing a clear set of beliefs regarding Jesus Christ. Plagued with assumptions that we can't still be called Christian if we don't offer quick (and correct!) answers to "Who is Jesus?," many of us try to suppress the doubts creeping inside us about the first-century rabbi from Palestine. You probably don't need to imagine yourself as one of the original disciples to feel sweat forming on your brow and butterflies in your stomach should someone turn to you right now and ask, "What about you, who do *you* say that Jesus is?"

Not long after Jesus's crucifixion, Christianity morphed into a religion centered on believing the exact right things about Jesus. Functioning like a speakeasy (but serving up eternal bliss in lieu of Sazeracs and old-fashioneds), over time the church extracted Jesus's question to his friends outside Caesarea Philippi and forged it into a secret passcode where only the faithful with the right answers get in. As a result, when we hear Jesus's question, "Who do you say that I am?," we assume he intended to quiz the disciples, testing that they knew the right answer. But I don't think that was Jesus's intent, nor should we imagine him holding up a ruler to you and me today to make sure we fit some Christologically perfect mold.

I want to liberate you from the oppressive notion that you *must* believe precise doctrinal statements about Jesus. To reject that notion is to unleash a power that will free you from those anxious moments when you realize you don't believe the same things about Jesus that you once did. Believing *in* Jesus, in who he was (or is), is not what matters most. Instead, God invites us to a posture of trust that the Way of Jesus offers both the ingredients of and the path to a flourishing, wholehearted, abundant life. Jesus embodied a radical belief that love, mercy, compassion, forgiveness, and grace could change the world. His mission involved calling people to live as he lived and think as he thought. It's taken me three decades, but ultimately I believe Jesus desired that people *trust* him, more so than trust *in* him.

The move toward progressive Christianity can include all sorts of terrain shifts regarding Jesus, far more than I can address in one chapter. Therefore, I'll hone in on just a few of the insights that have helped me most as I've stumbled through my Shift. Mainly, they have to do with reorienting our assumptions around what Jesus might expect from us, hence the story of Jesus asking his friends, "Who do you say that I am?" From this, we'll discover what Jesus isn't looking for (a correct answer), what he is looking for (us to do our own inner work), and what I think matters most as far as how Jesus hopes we understand him (stay tuned).

First, I want to take you on a tour through my evolving responses to the question, "What do I think about Jesus?"

MY EVOLVING JOURNEY WITH JESUS

On the heels of turning five, I decided the time had come. Moments after my dad tucked me in on the top bunk, I hollered his name back down the hall. He returned, flustered at what I must want now. I sprung to a sitting position and declared, "I'm ready to accept Jesus into my heart!"

Now, if this happened in my home today with any of my four boys, in addition to questioning where such an idea came from, I would assume they were pulling out yet one more card in their attempts to delay bedtime. Having already asked for a drink of water, a new and improved stuffed animal, and nighttime snug-snugs (our family's term for snuggling), they now think they can put off sleep by appealing to some cosmic transaction involving the admittance of a dead Jewish guy's ghost into their hearts. However, my dad—good fourth-generation Baptist that he was—delighted in such a delay. After all, five minutes of lost sleep is a small price to pay for escaping the flames of eternal torment. He flipped on the light and led me through a version of what we called the Sinner's Prayer.[1] Not that it made sense to me as a five-year-old, but in my short time on Earth, I'd evidently heard enough Sunday school lessons to pick up on the importance of such a prayer. Thus began my journey with Jesus.

Growing up, I identified as Christian because, in addition to praying the prayer at five years old, that's how my white, American, middle-class parents raised me. If you would've asked me anytime between the ages of five and fifteen, "Who do you say Jesus is?," I would've responded with something like, "He's my personal savior." At some point, I also learned that Jesus sat in the middle of this mysterious God triangle as the second person in the Trinity. So, not only was Jesus my personal savior, but I grew up learning that he was God, too.

The summer I turned seventeen, I tagged along on a trip to a conference in Southern California, unexpectedly altering the course of my life. The conference trained high schoolers to do street witnessing, and there on the sandy shores of Huntington Beach, while questioning surfers about the state of their souls, I discovered a desire (or "calling," as I named it) for full-time ministry— transforming me from a nominal Christian to the oversaved version of myself I will discuss in detail in chapter 9. Jesus became the Lord of my life as I committed to follow his teachings and pledged to become a pastor.

---

1   If you're unfamiliar, this is when a person prays to God and acknowledges being a sinner, asks for forgiveness, confesses a belief that Jesus died on the cross and rose from the dead, and then invites Jesus to come into their heart. The goal of many Christians is not only to say this prayer for themselves, but to get as many others to say it as possible.

Two years out of college, fresh with a degree in pastoral ministry and working as an associate worship pastor at a church in Salem, Oregon, I started reading books my Baptist college professors never would have included on their syllabi, thereby expanding my appreciation for Jesus beyond the limited scope of my familial heritage. I learned more about the central component of Jesus's teaching, a.k.a. the kingdom of God. Up to that point, I believed the kingdom of God (or "of heaven," as the Gospel of Matthew calls it) served as just another way to say "life after death." But at twenty-four years old, I came to see how Jesus cared about life here and now, and that his prayer involved God's will being done on Earth. Had you asked me then, "Who do you say that Jesus is?," my response might have been, "He's the inaugurator of the kingdom."

A few years later, Kate and I moved just outside Phoenix to join a young, fast-growing evangelical church where I added another layer to my answer for "Who is Jesus?" The lead pastor of our church saw everything through a lens of social justice, revealing to me for the first time how Jesus's message focused on the margins of society. I learned how the kingdom prioritizes the forgotten and privileges the outcast, the littlest, the lost, and the least. As a collection of stories and poems from marginalized people, the Bible testifies to a God who stands on the side of the oppressed. So, as I approached my thirtieth birthday, I would've described Jesus as "the liberator of the oppressed."

Fast-forward and, after getting fired from two churches in the span of two years,[2] and with most of my conservative beliefs firmly deconstructed, my wife and I decided to start a new progressive Christian church in San Diego. Our community consisted of people with a wide range of religious backgrounds and beliefs. Had you asked me at thirty-two who I thought Jesus was, about the only thing

---

2 You can read all about that lovely story in my book *UnClobber*.

I could've offered was, "Jesus is the embodiment of the Way." I took this to mean that living like Jesus seemed to be the best way to live. I would talk about the life and teachings of Jesus as empowering people to come fully alive and experience all of what it means to be human. I would talk about forgiveness being better than revenge, of peace being better than war, of love being better than hate, and so on.

Today, should Jesus ask me "Who do you say that I am?," I would answer much, much slower. Most days I might even go with "I don't know." Don't misunderstand me—in the twenty years since I gave my life to the calling of ministry, I have not let up on the gas of seeking after God and learning about Jesus. It's just that nowadays I know more about what I *don't* know than about what I do. If pressed, I'd probably say Jesus is the illuminator of love, as gushy and esoteric as that sounds. Someone who shows us what unconditional and sacrificial love looks like. He very well may be more than that, but he is at least that for me.

When I take a step back and summarize the evolution of my journey with Jesus, an interesting shape emerges. You can trace my trajectory from a small, personalized perspective of Jesus as someone who exists solely for my benefit to something much larger and more universal. What began as a very granular and specific sense of Jesus's identity grew over time to something nuanced, expansive, and inclusive. You could envision it like an upside-down funnel.

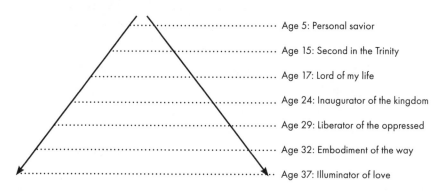

Age 5: Personal savior
Age 15: Second in the Trinity
Age 17: Lord of my life
Age 24: Inaugurator of the kingdom
Age 29: Liberator of the oppressed
Age 32: Embodiment of the way
Age 37: Illuminator of love

Now, if you take a big picture of church history, identifying the various ways it has responded to Jesus's question in the last two thousand years, I'm fascinated by how the trajectory is almost an exact inverse of mine. What started out as a message for all people, prophetically announced by Jesus, the roaming rabbi from up north, evolved (or rather, devolved) into a narrowly defined set of doctrines, varying between thousands of different denominations. Throughout church history, both Jesus's identity and his universal message of love endured centuries of modification, being reduced in the end to not much more than a person's entry ticket into heaven when they die.

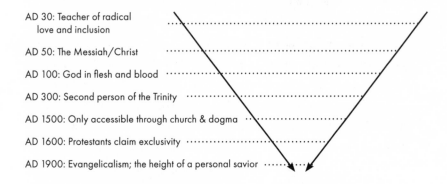

AD 30: Teacher of radical love and inclusion

AD 50: The Messiah/Christ

AD 100: God in flesh and blood

AD 300: Second person of the Trinity

AD 1500: Only accessible through church & dogma

AD 1600: Protestants claim exclusivity

AD 1900: Evangelicalism; the height of a personal savior

WHEN DID WE GET IT RIGHT?

These contrasting trajectories illuminate two helpful insights.

First, I would argue that we get closer to the heart and message of Jesus when our beliefs expand to include more people in the family of God. Any statements of belief about Jesus that result in narrowness and exclusivity fundamentally push against the trajectory Jesus initiated.

Second, both trajectories illustrate a vast breadth of responses to Jesus's question, "Who do you say that I am?" In my own journey and throughout church history, beliefs about Jesus have changed, grown, and evolved. If you mapped out your own journey, you would likely see similar evidence of growth and change. What kinds of change, or in what direction you moved, is hardly the point. Simply observe the normalcy of such change.

This raises an important question: Assuming for the moment that correct beliefs about Jesus are indeed of ultimate importance, where and when on the timeline—of either yours, mine, or the Christian church's—would we find the absolute best and most correct response to "Who is Jesus?" Was Christianity most accurate during Jesus's life and teaching, or maybe a couple decades later, when Paul entered the picture? What about when the church divided over the Trinity, or divided again over what transpires with the bread and wine during Communion? Do Catholics have Jesus more right, or do Protestants? And which of the thousands of denominations have the best response to "Who do you say that I am?" If there exists, as a matter of cosmic fact, a single correct answer to that question, then who gets to decide when and where over the past two thousand years that correct answer developed?

Or, perhaps the whole idea of there being a correct belief about the identity of Jesus needs to die so that something new can emerge.

In my own life, I am not prepared to look back and say to my seventeen-year-old self, "You were wrong about how you understood Jesus." I believe my response "Jesus is the Lord of my life" was the best I could've hoped for at that time, and I would say the same for every step of my transformation along the way. Sure, I think my current ideas of Jesus reflect deeper and more well-rounded insights than ever before, but I've witnessed too much change in my own life to plant an Ebenezer in my current answer "Jesus is the illuminator of love." At age thirty-seven, in the words of Saint Paul, I have not yet arrived (Phil 3:12). Instead of feeling great anxiety, however, I choose to relax into the rhythm of death and resurrection even as it relates to beliefs about Jesus, trusting once again that getting it right is not what it's all about.

Once we can step away from seeing Jesus's interaction with his disciples around his identity (recorded in Mark 8, Matthew 16, and Luke 9) as a theological inquiry into the rightness of belief, some profound and valuable insights rise to the surface.

REBUKING PROSELYTIZATION

We live in a society obsessed with getting noticed. No good deed goes untweeted. Furthermore, artists and influencers must fawn for more fans and followers, because the size of a person's platform directly correlates with publishing deals, brand sponsorships, and access to greater audiences. Unless you're Banksy, an obscured identity equals career suicide. Which makes it all the more shocking when, after Peter shared his thoughts on the matter ("You are the Christ"), Jesus responded by ordering "them to not tell anyone about him" (Mark 8:30 CEB). Needless to say, if Jesus lived today, his indifference toward platform size, and worse, his efforts to remain opaque to the masses, wouldn't even garner him fifteen minutes of fame—let alone trending status or the blue check mark of legitimacy.

Neither confirming nor denying the accuracy of Peter's response, Jesus cared most that his friends kept their thoughts to themselves. If Jesus desired people to correctly believe in him, then he would not have deliberately derailed his disciples from spreading the news. Yet, in each gospel account of this story, Jesus applied this strange lid of secrecy.

Seeing as how the church has made its mission telling the world that Jesus is the son of God and obsessively inviting people to believe in him, one wouldn't be faulted for assuming that later in Jesus's life he removed said lid of secrecy. When I used to come across these moments of Jesus saying "Don't tell anyone," I always assumed that somewhere down the road he reversed the order. A survey of the gospels reveals no such about-face, however. Never did Jesus turn to his friends and say, "Okay, *now* you can go tell people about my identity and to believe in me."[3] Not only did Jesus never reverse his directive, but an examination of the Greek where Jesus "ordered them to not tell anyone about him" reveals an even more powerful response.

In English, verse 30 gets translated as, "Jesus *ordered* them not to tell anyone about him" (CEB), "he *strictly charged* them to tell no one about him" (ESV), and "Jesus *warned* them not to tell anyone about him" (NIV). The Greek word translated as ordered/charged/warned is *epitimao*. Almost every one of the thirty-plus times *epitimao* shows up in the New Testament, translators go with the plainest meaning of the word, *to rebuke*. When Jesus rebukes the wind and the waves, when he rebukes demons, and when he rebukes Peter for trying to stop him, each time the Greek word used was *epitimao*. Four times, however, translators do not translate *epitimao* as rebuke. All four instances occur when Jesus instructs his disciples not to tell people about him. In those contexts, translators soften *epitimao* with words such as *ordered* or *charged*.

Pause to consider how much more potent Jesus's response to Peter and the others becomes when we hear it as he "rebuked them" with instruction to tell no one.

What people believed about or thought of Jesus simply didn't matter to him. He did not come to proclaim himself. His

---

3 You might object, "Hey, what about the Great Commission?" At the end of Matthew's Gospel, Jesus told his disciples, "Therefore go and make disciples of all nations, baptizing them in the name of the Father and of the Son and of the Holy Spirit, and teaching them to obey everything I have commanded you" (Matt 28:19–20 NIV). Look closely, and you don't find Jesus saying, "Tell people to believe in me," or "Make sure people know I'm the Christ." The disciples were tasked with emulating Jesus by making disciples. Getting more and more people to "obey everything" Jesus commanded. Which, as we've noted, was about how we treated our neighbor and loved our enemy, not about specific beliefs regarding Jesus's identity.

proclamations always pointed hearers to the kingdom of God and to the manifestation of God's will on Earth—most clearly seen in how we treat one another. Love for others revealed the mark of discipleship, not doctrinal belief (John 13:35). As the movement of the Way grew from scattered disciples at the cross to gathered disciples post-resurrection to organized house-churches in Jerusalem, Samaria, and beyond, and then to the Constantine-approved state religion, things radically shifted. The message disconnected from—and became secondary to—the messenger. Jesus went from being the proclaimer to the proclaimed. Whereas he spent his brief ministry calling followers, the religion that bears his name focused on churning out worshippers.

Instead of learning to live like Jesus, we've settled for a simple gesture of believing in him.

WITHIN IS BETTER

The Gospel of Matthew adds an interesting detail to this story—a detail that, for me, helps to ground the ever-growing and constantly changing ideas, perceptions, and beliefs we might have about Jesus. The GPS in your car or on your phone provide a confidence that no matter where you go or which path you take, you'll be okay. Before rebuking the disciples not to tell anyone, the affirmation Jesus gave Peter in Matthew 16 is kind of like that.

> He [Jesus] said, "And what about you? Who do you say that I am?" Simon Peter said, "You are the Christ, the son of the living God." Then Jesus replied, "Happy are you, Simon, son of Jonah, *because no human has shown this to you.* Rather, my Father who is in heaven has shown you." (Matt 16:15–18, emphasis mine)

Again, notice that Jesus didn't exactly affirm that Peter got the answer right. That wasn't the point. What Jesus did do, though, should slash most church's evangelism budgets in half.

Upon hearing Peter's belief that Jesus was the Christ, Jesus said, "Happy are you . . . *because no human has shown this to you.*" For Jesus, the best part of Peter's response had little to do with accuracy and everything to do with the fact that he arrived at his conclusion on his own. When Jesus says, "my Father who is in heaven has shown you," he's naming that the conviction in Peter's heart and mind—that Jesus was the Christ—came from within him.

Sometimes we won't learn life's most important lessons through a book, or podcast, or sermon, or coffee with a friend, or on the couch of a therapist. Sometimes, the most important lessons we learn well up from within us. Oh, that we might awaken to the still small voice buried deep within, trusting that maybe it knows what it's talking about. After all, isn't that what Jesus did? And isn't that what pissed off the religious leaders so much? "Where do you get your authority from?" they often demanded. In those days, you had to study from an already established rabbi, and *then* you could regurgitate *their* teachings. But along came Jesus, whose wisdom came from deep within himself. He minted his own credibility and the existing power structures blew (whatever would be the first-century equivalent of) their gaskets.

Peter presented this wisdom from within as he threw caution to the wind and went for it. If you're gonna go down, go down swinging—right, Pete? So what if everyone else believed Jesus to be a resurrected old prophet; Peter embodied true courage as he listened to what his heart told him. Jesus recognized Peter's bold step of faith, loved it, and affirmed it. *You came to that conclusion on your own and were unafraid to say so? Incredible! Well done!*

Even if Christian leaders can make a case that having the correct belief about his identity mattered to Jesus (and I don't think they can), one still must acknowledge that Jesus preferred it when someone came to such a conclusion by themselves, not as a result of a fancy gospel tract, flashy preaching series, or a community BBQ with a captivating evangelist.

The irony is not lost on me that one of the most pivotal moments in my spiritual life occurred while engaging in an activity Jesus prohibited. I spent a week as a teenager randomly pestering tourists in Southern California about the eternal importance of believing in Jesus as their savior, even though two thousand years ago Jesus rebuked his disciples for the very same thing. Yet, witnessing to strangers on the beaches of L.A. changed the course of my life and led me to a deeper relationship with God through Jesus. I can't help but think that happened in spite of my evangelistic efforts, not because of them.

WHY DID JESUS ASK THIS QUESTION?

To assume Jesus's greatest concern—both then and now—begins and ends with what people believe about him fundamentally misses the point of his teachings. Such an assumption takes us in a narrow, excluding trajectory away from his heart and mission. There's one final observation I want to make from Mark 8 to rehumanize the story and discover a universal insight into the human condition. One that can bring us all together, not divide us over precarious fault lines of so many competing beliefs around Jesus.

It begins with a question: If Jesus wasn't quizzing his disciples (or us) about their Christology, then why might he have asked them those two questions?

In the two chapters leading up to that moment outside Caesarea Philippi, Jesus endured the following:

- His cousin, John the Baptist, died (6:14)
- He desired isolation from the crowds (6:31)
- He struggled through another episode of his disciples' lack of understanding (6:51)
- A crowd recognized and mobbed him (6:53)

- ✦ Pharisees put him to the test (7:1)
- ✦ A Greek woman challenged his theology (7:28)
- ✦ He healed a blind man and ordered secrecy, but people blabbed anyway (7:36)
- ✦ More pharisees called him out and demanded proof (8:11)
- ✦ His disciples once again revealed confusion about it all (8:21)

When taken together, we get a picture of someone who is constantly giving himself, constantly doubted and questioned, and constantly in demand and sought after. All the while, he is mourning the loss of his beloved cousin, yet not given the space to fully feel and express his emotions. In other words, Jesus was exhausted, frustrated, lonely, misunderstood, emotionally torn, and probably questioning his calling and sense of self. (This might explain the comical story in Mark 8:22–26 where Jesus healed a blind man . . . but it took him two tries! Is it too heretical to suggest that such exhaustion, loneliness, and self-doubt would shake *anyone's* confidence?) All these events lead up to Jesus asking his friends one afternoon, "What are people saying about me? What do *you* say about me?"

Taking a page out of Peter's playbook, I want to share what I've discovered from deep within as I've reflected on this story. Reading it in its broader context in Mark, and holding it up to my own life, it makes sense why Jesus might've checked in with his friends in this way.

HELP ME SEE ME

For the first three decades of my life, I constructed various images of myself to project to the world. Instead of learning about and discovering who Colby is, I spent years burying my true self under layers and layers of the smart guy, the funny guy, the attractive guy, the sports guy, the has-it-all-together guy, the witty guy, and the guy-with-all-the-answers guy . . . to name a few. The past several years have been a painful yet liberating process of peeling back all those layers and getting to know the real Colby, free from the masks I wear and the false selves I project.

The work of self-discovery, necessary and good though it may be, is also exhausting, frustrating, and at times very lonely. I often feel misunderstood—both by myself and by others. And I've absolutely found myself questioning my calling and purpose in life more than once.

Part of my journey involved asking questions like, "Who do people say that I am?" This question functioned as a road sign pointing me toward the false images I projected in the world. The most intense and revealing question, though, happened when I turned toward someone who knew me better than anyone else—better even than I know myself—and asked, "Kate, who do *you* say that I am?" My wife has been able to speak truth to me in ways no one else can. She has brought life into these dry bones, calling out the best parts of me and helping me see my true self while I stumble along in the dark.

Such is the gift of honest, vulnerable, and loving relationships. Whether it's with one person (such as a spouse, partner, or sibling) or a group (such as a church community or small circle of friends), there exists immense power in using other people's eyes to see ourselves more clearly.

Through ads, movies, and other media, the world constantly bombards us with lies about who we are: unhappy without this product, not as beautiful as that actress, six steps away from the perfect relationship. Coworkers, random people on the street, and sometimes even our own families fill our heads with narratives about who they think we are: lazy, ugly, worthless, annoying, arrogant. The voices inside our heads rarely do us any favors as we bury ourselves with thoughts of being stupid, the worst, unlovable, and a failure. But the voice of those who love us can call us back to ourselves: you are powerful, fierce, compassionate, and kind. You are loved and you are lovable, just as you are.

Jesus was human, full stop. His brief public ministry had to have taken a toll on him. I get the sense that Jesus might have asked his closest friends to reflect back to him what they saw because he fully immersed himself in the draining and lonely work of loving people unconditionally, challenging the powers of the day, and calling people back to a life centered in love of God, neighbor, and self. If he didn't need to pause occasionally and fill up on love and affirmation from those who loved him most, those who believed in him even when he struggled to believe in himself, then he's honestly not someone I can relate to. But this story in the gospels illustrates why I keep trusting Jesus, and why I keep coming back to a belief that he is worthy of following and imitating.

SO WHO DO YOU SAY JESUS IS?

Some of the scariest steps on the path toward becoming a progressive Christian involve wobbling over our beliefs around Jesus. In our hopes to preserve the Christian part of us, we fear looking too closely. If only we could trust that maybe it's not about what we believe about Jesus. Maybe whatever you think now is just fine, as will be whatever you think a year from now. Believing *in* Jesus isn't the point. It never was. Rather, may we *believe* Jesus that giving our lives to the way of love, peace, mercy, and compassion is what matters most.

Instead of hearing Jesus ask "Who do you say that I am?" to test whether you're really a Christian, may you hear in those words an echo of what it truly means to be human. May you hear in those words permission to be exhausted, lonely, and confused. May you hear in those words a way forward, where you build relationships with people you trust who can speak truth in your life when you need it most.

Who is Jesus? According to his own words, he is the human one. I think the more we lean into *that*, accepting his own description of himself and receiving him in his full humanity, the more it becomes an invitation to accept our own humanity. The importance of this question lies not in a need to have the correct theological belief in order to secure a mansion in the sky. Rather, in seeing the full humanity in Jesus, we wake up to the full humanity in us. Fully loved by God, just like Jesus.

"Who do you say that I am?" Jesus asks.

We reply, "You are the human one, the loved child of God."

Jesus smiles and says, "And so are you. *How great is that?*"

Inspired by Old, Dusty Books

What to Do with the Bible

I don't want to add up how many hours I spent playing *Mario Kart* as a kid. Good gravy, I might have a PhD by now had I spent my weekends and after-school hours more prudently. Still, I have no regrets. Even now, as I type, if someone showed up with a Super Nintendo and challenged me to a 150cc Mushroom Cup Grand Prix, sorry, dear reader, I'd leave you in a heartbeat.

If I didn't know a course yet, my strategy involved choosing a small and nimble kart (Toadstool FTW!) for tight turning and quick acceleration out of crashes. But once I had the course memorized and could anticipate each turn or obstacle, I'd pick Donkey Kong every time. No kart could match him for pure speed.

The newest version of *Mario Kart* offers twenty-three different items hiding in those spinning question-mark boxes, but in the original version—the one that robbed me of a PhD—there were six. In my opinion, the banana peel gets the prize as the most undervalued weapon. I didn't fully appreciate its potential until I realized that if you held Up on the directional pad while pressing the A button, you could launch the peel over racers ahead of you, ostensibly creating an obstacle for your opponents out of thin air. When timed properly, whether dropping it behind or launching it forward, the banana peel is a dangerous weapon to foil the progress of your friends and family.

Kind of like the Bible.

WEAPONIZING THE BIBLE

Friction with Scripture is another significant obstacle when becoming a progressive Christian. Nothing stops you quicker in your tracks than when those closest to you respond to your newfound expression of faith with, "Well, the Bible says . . ." Weaponized like the banana peel, many of us have endured friends and family members who harnessed the power of the Bible in their attempts to prevent us from further advancing down the path toward progressive Christianity.

Who among us hasn't cringed through a multiple-swipes-long stream of copy/paste Bible verses posted on our Facebook page in a feeble effort to show us the error of our ways? Or rolled our eyes at emails passive-aggressively closed with nothing but a verse reference casually dropped at the end, forcing us to look it up on our own, stung by its implication (i.e., Matt 26:41, 2 Chr 7:14, or 1 Tim 4:1). Or who hasn't been in the middle of telling your dad about a recent Rob Bell podcast or Jen Hatmaker book when he suddenly cuts the conversation short and walks off mumbling, "For the time will come when people will not put up with sound doctrine. Instead, to suit their own desires, they will gather around them a great number of teachers to say what their itching ears want to hear," as though he memorized 2 Timothy 4:3 for such a time as this.

As you embark on your Shift, no one can prepare you for how many Bible verses well-intentioned people will hurl your way. Your exit will trigger all sorts of insecurity among your old church, family, and friends. In their fear, they will attempt to pull you back by appealing to Paul in Romans or Jesus in Matthew, as though one last verse might do the trick. I'm not sure there exists a more unique and perverse pain than when the people you love forge the words (you used to love) into a weapon aimed to shame you, accuse you, or otherwise justify their troubling behavior toward you. For all the times and ways this might have happened to you, I am sorry. It is wrong and you did not (and do not) deserve it. If leaving conservative Christianity wasn't already motivated in part by a sense of disillusionment regarding the Bible, then I'm sure having it weaponized against you soured your feelings toward it even more.

In high school, I remember returning to the intersection where, just days earlier, a brutal car accident nearly took my life. My heart raced and my stomach lurched as we pulled up to the exact location where the flatbed tow truck (*which was also towing a car!*) T-boned my shiny, red 1988 Nissan Pulsar. When you open a Bible these days, or—like many people in my church have told me—sit in church when your pastor reads a passage aloud, you might experience a similar sort of PTSD. The struggle is real, especially if your exit from conservative Christianity involved getting kicked out, with Bible verses utilized as justification for your shunning.

If you never pick up the Bible again, I don't blame you.

THE BIBLE AND PROGRESSIVE CHRISTIANITY

On the other hand, maybe you haven't completely sworn off the Bible . . . yet. But things are clearly different now. In your previous life, you might have read it daily, highlighted your favorite verses, and looked forward to hearing your pastor unpack the original meaning of the text. Now, you can't recall off the top of your head where in the house your Bible sits—assuming you still have one. Questions such as "What even is the Bible?" and "Who cares what old dudes wrote thousands of years ago?" and "Can it really offer any value for me?" swirl in your mind like the last piece of cereal refusing to be scooped up by the spoon.

Even if you escaped having the Bible weaponized against you, you still probably don't feel the same way about it as you once did. No longer do you reach for it when hard times come, as the words that once brought comfort now stir only questions. Nor do ancient customs function any longer as your moral compass, for you realize that twenty-first-century issues such as climate change and tax reform weren't on the minds of Stone Age philosophers as they mused on tribal warfare etiquette or which animal sacrifice covers which transgression.

Some days you might feel resentful that many of the beliefs you no longer hold can still nonetheless be reasonably supported and defended by this verse or that passage (as I'm sure your old Bible study group won't let you forget). It's just that you've come to believe either (1) those verses have been grossly misunderstood or misinterpreted, and/or (2) regardless of what the verse says, you know deep in your bones that it can't be right. Every part of your conscience feels violated when, for instance, women are denied leadership roles in the church—verses about submission and silence be damned.

You're not foolish for feeling frustrated with the Bible. Nor are you alone. Most people I've encountered who have experienced the Shift feel far removed from the days when they took for granted that the word of God provided everything needed for life.

Figuring out how (or if) the Bible still plays a role in our lives as we become a progressive Christian ranks as one of the more confusing parts of the Shift.

I don't have any easy answers. Yet, even though my posture toward the Bible has changed dramatically, I still believe it offers time-tested witness to some of life's deepest and most powerful truths. And if we're open to it, the wisdom of the past can provide light, companionship, and insight for the journey ahead.

THE PERFECT WORD OF GOD

The first thing concerned Christians question when you start shedding the clothes of conservative Christianity is your commitment to the Bible. This usually comes by way of a form (metaphorically speaking) containing two boxes: one labeled "Inerrant" and the other "Infallible," followed by a request that you still check both. In their minds, failure to do so signals that you truly have abandoned the faith. Yet, it's fully possible (even preferable) to drop these two commitments *and* still be a Christian who learns from, is energized by, and holds the Bible as a sacred work of art. So, here's what Cheryl, your old choir director, means when she looks at you aghast and says, "Well, don't you believe the Bible is the perfect *word of God?*"

First, the term *inerrant* means "without error." To say the Bible is inerrant means its facts are accurate, it does not contradict itself, and everything inside it—if interpreted correctly—is absolutely true. Most progressive Christians reject the inerrancy of Scripture, either explicitly or implicitly. This often happens when we discover how areas of science such as evolutionary biology and archeology directly contradict either the historical facts in the Bible or a literal reading of the text (i.e., the creation accounts in Genesis 1–2). With regards to contradictions in the Bible, I recall the incredible feats of mental gymnastics required to try to square obviously different accounts in the gospels of things like Jesus's genealogy, birth story, and what took place that first Easter morning. Maintaining that the Bible is without error simply became an untenable position for many of us who left conservative Christianity.

Second, the term *infallibility* in its strictest sense means "incapable of making a mistake." Most Christians use the term to mean that the Bible is reliable and trustworthy and will not lead you astray. Like inerrancy, progressive Christians can't accept the infallibility of the Bible seeing as how the church used Scripture to justify slavery, the subjugation of women, and the oppression of LGBTQ people. Those three efforts all had "strong biblical support," yet they are also some of the grossest stains on the history of the church. Obviously, one can follow the literal words of the Bible and still be led to disastrous and inhumane outcomes, rendering *infallibility* an idea one cannot in good conscience use in conjunction with the Bible.

I have held on to, however, a third *I* word used to describe the Bible, though I asterisk the hell out of it. I'm referring to *inspired*, and even though I don't mean it in the same way I once did, I nonetheless still consider the Bible to be a divinely inspired collection of ancient letters, stories, and poems. Allow me to explain.

DIVINELY INSPIRED

Along with most of your conservative friends and family, I used to understand divine inspiration like this: God, as a super being up/ out there, exerted "his" actual thoughts and words *into* and *through* the men who composed the works that came together as the Bible. To say the Bible was divinely inspired, in other words, was to say that the very ink on the papyrus flowed directly from the mind of God via the Holy Spirit. Sure, theologians give space for the unique personalities of each biblical writer to shine, but the bottom line remains: God beamed words to Earth via meat-puppet vessels known as Moses, Jeremiah, Peter, Paul, and so on.

I no longer find that a compelling or plausible account of how the Bible came to be. Now when I think about the Bible as inspired by God, I think about God as described earlier in chapter 4. Not so much a being out there who exercises an option to control beings down here, but more like an Event, an Ultimate Reality, a Source from which creative goodness flows and gives witness.

If you imagine God as the highest truth, the deepest beauty, and the greatest good, then whatever work of art in our space and time illuminates what is true, beautiful, or good must therefore point to God. And not only point to God, as though art is the tip of an iceberg merely testifying to an even greater amount of ice beyond itself, but you can also imagine art (truth/beauty/goodness) flowing *out of* God as a product of the divine at work. God can therefore be conceived of as both the ultimate reality of the iceberg below *and* the water itself by which the iceberg comes to be at all. God: both source and object of artistic expression.

So, am I saying that the Bible sits rather unexceptionally alongside other inspired works of art such as Michelangelo's *David*, Mozart's *Don Giovanni*, and every time LeBron James takes the floor? Well, no and yes. Great inspired works of art must also *come from* and *point to* God. There's no other option, as I see it. (Not unlike at the end of *The Last Battle*, when Aslan welcomes the pagan Emeth into heaven by saying, "Child, all the service thou hast done to Tash, I account as service done to me.") But clearly not all inspired works are created equal. Some capture *more* of the ultimate reality. Some reflect *more* of the highest truth, deepest beauty, and greatest good than others.

Further, not all works inspired by God offer the same value in terms of their capacity to transform a person's life or aid them in coming more alive. When I say that God inspired the Bible, I am naming its deep potential to reveal beneficial truths about the human experience in such a way that empowers us to change for the better. I wholeheartedly agree with 2 Timothy 3:16–17, which says scripture "is inspired by God and is useful for teaching, for showing mistakes, for correcting, and for training character, so that the person who belongs to God can be equipped to do everything that is good." Yes, yes, and yes! The Bible need be neither infallible nor inerrant for it to be useful for teaching, training character, and equipping us to do good.

Yes, the Bible has errors and contradictions, and it has been used to justify grotesque actions. Humanity has often been guilty of using good things to justify bad deeds. At the same time, my progressive sensibilities are not threatened by maintaining a conviction that the Bible still possesses immense value. I believe that this collection of ancient poems (written in an attempt to articulate humanity's experience with God), letters (composed to the earliest churches in an effort to organize and spread a new type of beloved community), and stories (passed on through oral tradition for hundreds of years before being collected, edited, and written down for future generations), all point to ultimate truth, beauty, and goodness as they flow from the depths of divine wisdom.

In other words, *inspired*.

FOUR TIPS FOR REAPPROACHING THE BIBLE

If you're interested in (or open to) integrating the Bible with your spiritual life, but are unsure how to do so (because you're still a bit unsure about the Bible in general), let me offer you four suggestions. I've found these principles immensely helpful in not only renewing my appreciation for the good book but unlocking a whole new way to interact with it.

1. READ THE BIBLE LITERATELY INSTEAD OF LITERALLY. In other words, if we miss that something is an allegory and read it as an historical record or ignore that a particular passage is poetry and read it as propositional truth statements, we'll be like my son using a butter knife to make a robot costume from a cardboard Amazon box. Wrong tool, wrong approach, and nothing but crude, disastrous results await. Reading the Bible literally is tempting as a simple and clear way to interact with the words on the page, and no doubt was the primary approach many of us grew up with, but it flattens all flavor and ignores any nuance. Taking the time to let the genres and the styles of the literature inform how we read and understand it can transform what these ancient letters, poems, and stories do in and for us. Which leads me to . . .

2. PLAY WITH THE TEXT. Oh, that Christians might learn from our Jewish heritage, which takes for granted that any given passage of Scripture might have room for dozens of different ways to see, understand, and live it. The goal is less about figuring out the right answer and more about the conversation dancing around the various ways the words make people light up. I used to read a story in the gospels and ask, "What exactly happened? What did it mean back then? What does it mean now?" Nowadays, I approach it in the same manner my friend Scott, an artist, challenges people to approach any work of art. Instead of asking "What does it mean?," we stand before it, hearts open, and ask, "What is this stirring up inside me?" Seen in this way, I've discovered Bible stories as mirrors that reflect me back to myself, or poems that articulate my own feelings of lament or jubilation. I've found layered in the letters to the early church Peter and Paul's exhaustion in trying to build spiritual communities, helping me feel like less of a failure when I think about how hard church planting is. Playing with the text gives us the freedom to receive such insights.

3. TAKE THE BEST AND LEAVE THE REST. Anyone who has ever tried to take the Bible seriously ends up picking and choosing which passages to emphasize and which to ignore. Admitting this is true is the first (and hardest) step. My previous conservative self, steeped in evangelical thought and action, followed the party line "We don't pick and choose! We believe every word of the Word." But I was simply ignorant to all the ways I was indeed picking and choosing. I recall the intense fear surrounding any suggestion that a particular verse or passage not be true, because in my conservative Christian world the Bible was an all-or-nothing book. But now I encourage people to let whatever parts of the Bible speak to or resonate with them do their thing. And if other parts or entire books do nothing for them, no worries! No need to force it. For example, when Paul writes in Colossians 3:18–4:1 about "wives submitting to their husbands" and "slaves obeying their masters," there are reasons abound to let such words fall to the wayside. And maybe, once we give ourselves permission not to take those words literally, and not to think they are God's design for how homes should function for all of history, other insights might emerge. Such as how Paul, in this passage, began with the culture's standard codes of conduct for households and then imagined what a transformed household might look like as a result of the teachings of Jesus. Yes, this passage as we read it now is backwards and archaic, yet for its time it was movement toward greater justice, equality, and love. Then we can ask questions like, "How might we, today, imagine elevating our own society's expectations of what a family should or should not look like?" Seen in this way, the Bible becomes "living" and "active" (Heb 4:12), with the potential to be a potent tool in manifesting the kingdom of God on Earth as it is in heaven.

4. USE LOVE AS YOUR HERMENEUTIC. *Hermeneutic* is a fancy word that means "how you interpret the Bible," sort of like the lens through which you see the text. Cartoonist David Hayward, whose website declares he creates "graffiti on the walls of religion," once drew a cartoon where Jesus says to a group of people, "The difference between me and you is you use Scripture to determine what love means and I use love to determine what Scripture means."[1] That's a hermeneutic of love. When I decided to let love be my hermeneutic—inspired by Jesus's continued insistence that the most important thing in life is love (for God, for self, for neighbor)— suddenly, I had the tool I needed to navigate these ancient stories, letters, and so on. Whatever this or that passage says or means or points to, if it's not greater wholeness and connection, and if the end result is not love, then it is just a noisy gong or a clanging cymbal.

HOW THE BIBLE STILL SPEAKS

I'm about as progressive as they come, and at the same time, the Bible still emerges as a source of great wisdom for me—even after dropping beliefs about the inerrancy of Scripture. Making these slight (but significant) tweaks in how I approach the Bible has freed me up to find God once again in Genesis, Mark, and Corinthians. Using this new approach, I want to share with you just a few ways that the Bible has deeply impacted me these past couple of years.

In the Bible I learned how practicing gratitude for the grace of the present moment rescues us from the misplaced nostalgia of yesterday and the needless anxiety around tomorrow. How did I learn this? Through the ancient Jewish legend of manna, the stories from Exodus that tell how God miraculously provided a breadlike substance for the Hebrew people and sustained them as they

---

1 David Hayward, "Love Versus the Bible," *Naked Pastor*, January 30, 2019, https://tinyurl.com/yyufckcv.

wandered the wilderness for forty years. The recently liberated slaves, upon running out of provisions, cried out in hunger and longed to go back to Egypt . . . *to be slaves again!* . . . but, hey, at least their bellies got filled. How often does our current pain blind us into longing for days gone by? At some point in your journey away from conservative Christianity, you may experience moments when you feel so lonely and sad that, even though it goes against everything you've come to believe, you find yourself wishing you could go back. You want to go back to your old church and old friends, because at least then you felt a part of something. God responds to this ache with manna, a temporary substance that cannot be stored, so it cannot be relied upon for future security. What manna does is ground you in the here and now, forcing you to pay attention to this moment. It is such mindfulness of the present that rescues us from nostalgia for the past and keeps us from getting anxious for the future. "Give us this day our daily bread," Jesus prayed. Today, here, now.

In the Bible is where I realized sometimes the wind, rain, and crashing waves don't scare me nearly as much as the calm *after* the storm. The gospels tell the story of when Jesus and the disciples were on a boat one evening and a storm hit, threatening to overwhelm them all. The disciples woke up a sleeping Jesus, who rolled over and ordered, "'Silence! Be still!' The wind settled down and there was a great calm" (Mark 4:39). I never noticed how Jesus then asked his friends "Why are you frightened?" (v. 40) only *after* the storm had passed. Sometimes I think we over-identify with our storm, our pain, our rotten situations in life. Sometimes, though it beats us down, we become comfortable as the victim of the raging storm. So much so that we're terrified—not of remaining in our pain—but at the prospect of healing. We might sabotage our own efforts to get better, frightened by a future freed from our pain. I cling to my victimhood because at least then, when people abandon me or let me down, I can nurse my wounds by saying, "See, I told you this would happen. People always let you down." Sad and lonely, sure, but also strangely comfortable and definitely predictable. I know the storm. It's the unknown calm that concerns me. Jesus then asked his friends, "Don't you have *pistis* yet?," and it echoes through the ancient pages as a challenge to me to remain open, trusting in the transforming power of God. It challenges me to trust that not only will the storm not kill me, but that on the other side of it I can survive the calm as well. Perhaps it's time for me to claim that the storm is over and get on with the business of healing and living.

In the Bible I discovered language to articulate how our true strength can never fully manifest without us first becoming undone. I discovered this in one of Paul's letters to the Corinthian church in which he bragged about his weaknesses and told the story of how God refused to relieve him of a thorn in his side. Paul heard from God the words, "My grace is enough for you, because power is made perfect in weakness" (2 Cor 12:9). Of course, I'd heard this verse countless times, but a couple years ago during a challenging season of coming to grips with my own humanity, where I peeled back many of the masks I referred to in the last chapter, I heard these words as though for the first time. "Power," which can mean *strength*, "is made perfect," which is to say *whole* or *complete*, "in weakness," which described perfectly my experience of coming to the end of my many false selves. There is a type of formation in character, a strengthening, that only comes on the other side of fully falling apart. I hate the falling apart, yet I can look back on those moments and see how they led me toward a life more whole, complete, connected, and beautiful. In hindsight, I can echo Paul's words, "Therefore, I'm all right with weaknesses, insults, disasters, harassments, and stressful situations for the sake of Christ, because when I'm weak, then I'm strong" (2 Cor 12:10).

A DUSTY, OLD GIFT

Ten years ago, I would've read those last three paragraphs and rolled my eyes, annoyed at the interpretations and offended by the loosey-goosey, esoteric, overly sentimental applications. I used to believe the Bible had one possible truth, one interpretation, one meaning for every verse, and the Christian's job was to study, memorize, understand, and live it. As a pastor and author, I'm clearly not opposed to studying the Bible or trying to understand it, but my posture toward what the Bible is (and is not) has completely shifted.

No, it's not a perfect account of history or a perfect recording of the voice of God declaring divine revelation for all time. No, it's not immune from leading us astray, nor does it hold all the answers for all of life's problems. Yes, it has been used to justify great harm toward many people. Yes, it can be triggering to hear old, familiar verses and phrases. As mentioned earlier, I completely understand if you need to leave the Bible behind altogether.

But when (or if) you're ready, you can hold the Bible in such a way that it frees you up to rediscover fresh insights, profound truths, and ancient wisdom within its pages. If you'd like, you might try pushing through your resistance to all the ways the Bible has been misused or leveraged to control and manipulate, and perhaps discover on the other end an openness to hear these words in a new light. Who knows what you might find?

I like to think of the Bible as this hard-fought gift that took thousands of years of psychological, emotional, and spiritual struggle in order to unearth some of the deepest truths of what it means to be human. And this gift, against all odds, now sits at my fingertips thanks to hundreds of years of men and women compiling, curating, and preserving such wisdom.

All complications and questions aside, millions of people have found this gift to be a lamp unto their feet and a light for their path. Seeing as how I often find myself stumbling around in the dark, perhaps I too might receive the gift of the light waiting to be discovered in these old, dusty books.

I Can't Stand Church...
Where Can I Find One?

What to Do with Your Love/Hate Relationship with Church

Some call me the Sherlock Holmes of progressive Christianity (okay, fine, no one has ever called me that). Still, like Holmes knowing John Watson is a wounded Afghanistan war doctor ("though at least partly psychosomatic"[1]) who is in therapy and at odds with his alcoholic brother merely by observing his appearance, gait, cell phone, and speech pattern, I've learned to recognize the signs of those who've experienced suffering at the hands of church and religion.

New people show up to our church every Sunday desperate for a safe place to be seen and loved. Taking a sizable risk, they

---

1 "A Study in Pink," in Sherlock, BBC, July 5, 2010.

walk through the doors daring to hope for a different kind of faith community. They often show up late, planning to slide in the back (unaware that no one at Sojourn shows up on time, so arriving fifteen minutes late probably still makes you early). They bob and weave through the various volunteers extending hospitality through hugs and handshakes, making eye contact only long enough so as not to appear rude. If they have kids, they might huddle in the back of the room, arms containing their sons and daughters like a hen protecting her chicks. They hope for a church their children might grow in, yet need it to be so different from those of their youth. Exhaustion leaks from each timid step as they eventually perch on the edge of a seat—near the exit, just in case. Maybe they stand when the music starts, maybe not. They want to sing along, but they also can't stomach it. Church music: one of many instigators of conflicting emotions when people try out church again after their Shift.

There they sit, surrounded by people laughing, hugging, crying, or otherwise honestly reflecting whatever state they're in, because at Sojourn we aim to shed all pretense. But they can't yet participate in such authenticity. Of course not; how could they? No matter how hard churches try, the temptation to show up in a Sunday smile insisting you are good and everything is fine permeates every assembly, congregation, and cathedral.

It will take a while before they believe that they are human, like everyone else, and that such a state is "supremely good" (Gen 1:31). After all, they've spent years in a codependent relationship with God, anxiously trying to manage God's feelings, desperate each day for the Good Cop God. They've never fully felt loved because in the back of their mind, they're haunted by the echoes of preachers gone by: "God cannot stand the sight of you because of your sin." So, when I or Kate stand up and insist, "You are a loved child of God, full stop!," they cock their head to the side like a curious dog, brow furrowed, drenched in skepticism. I've seen it a hundred times, and it makes so much sense.

Yet, they're here. Every week. New faces, suspiciously eager (or is it optimistically uncertain?). Perhaps you can relate, identifying with the tension in what feels like a dubious hope mixed with some skeptical yearning. You're scared to try church again, yet simultaneously thirsting for community, ritual, and connection. You approach faith communities with the push/pull of Mumford & Sons: "And my head told my heart, 'Let love grow.' But my heart told my head, 'This time no.'"[2]

If this paradoxical state describes you, you are entirely normal. We are relational beings, so you're not weak and it's no moral failure to want to find a church again, even though your rational mind can name all the reasons why it's a bad idea. On the one hand, you swear you're over the whole church thing because fool me twice, shame on me. On the other hand, you struggle to ignore this yearning deep inside that not only intuits there's more to life than atoms and molecules and pizza and paychecks, but you want to explore this unseen depth alongside others within the electricity of community, where you can see and be seen, know and be known.

Once a week I receive the same kind of email from someone in some part of the country. It begins with "I can't stand church" and ends with "Do you know one in my city I could try?"

HOW CHURCHES STEWARD GOD

Though it has battered me and left me for dead—twice—I still believe the church holds enormous potential to connect what has been severed, to unify what has been divided, and to heal what

---

2 Mumford & Sons, "Winter Winds," *Sigh No More*, Eastcote Studios, 2009.

has been damaged. No one disputes the injury perpetrated by religious groups of all shapes and sizes. But the vision of those first churches—to build diverse communities centered on radical love and hospitality for the sake of reconciling the world back to God and to each other—still captures my imagination. I suspect, considering you're reading this book, you share at least some version of my love-hate relationship with church. Part of the problem stems from how churches have lost the plot when it comes to their role in stewarding God.

Many progressive Christians sour on the idea of church because it claims proprietary access to God, as though it were a religious device made by Apple. You might have been sold a bill of goods that promised the presence of God on the corner of Elm and Twenty-Second, with fine print that seriously doubts your ability to find the divine anywhere else. Rarely do churches explicitly say so, but the message comes across loud and clear: come *here* to experience God (as opposed to, say, the beach or brunch). How quickly we've forgotten the words spoken by Stephen shortly before the rage of religious leaders led to his stoning: "The most high doesn't live in houses built by human hands" (Acts 7:48).

The story of how the temple veil rent in two upon Jesus's last breath (Matt 27:51) illustrates that humanity's attempt to segregate the sacred from the profane is and always will be a foolish endeavor. There is no God *inside* the holy of holies, other than the exact same one who always resided *outside* it as well.

* * *

I used to read that story as a transitional moment from the old covenant to the new, as though the halftime show just ended, the coaches have evaluated how the first half went, and now everyone runs out of the tunnel with a new game plan for the next two quarters. I believed humans, prior to Jesus, could only access God's presence through the temple, the sacrifices, and the mediation of the priests. Yet, thanks to the cross, the veil has been torn and, like a Niffler escaping Newt Scamander's suitcase, God gets to roam free. A new era dawns where humanity can experience God anywhere.

However, now I get the sense that humanity has always misunderstood the divine anytime we think we can contain, control, or codify it. The beauty of the veil being torn is not that now God is free, but that we got to see how God was not in there to begin with. Therefore, humanity is liberated from the entire enterprise of such religious illusions. The separated god, the absent god, and the just-do-these-few-things-first god all need to die, so that rising from the ashes can emerge the God who's "never far from us" and "in whom we live and move and have our being" (Acts 17:28).

The institution of church likewise needs its gods to die. There is no god under the steeple, there is no god upon the altar, there is no god in the candles, the incense, the fog machine or moving lights. Much of Christian worship barely differs from the temples Jesus cleansed, and in our arrogance we've built cathedrals believing that though God may no longer dwell in the holy of holies, surely he'll enjoy our glorious five-star accommodations.

We do not *go* to church to find God. We do not *go* to church to fill up on God, like a Costco trip to restock for the month (or, in our family, more like the week). The pews, chairs, stage, stained-glass windows—these are not the accoutrements of the sacred, as though the couch in your living room or the Miles Davis playing at Starbucks are not. The church has failed us by perpetuating liturgies and rituals designed to manufacture a sacred world above and against the more ordinary "secular" things, rather than illuminate the sacredness of all we call secular. The bread and the cup are not special because in them God shows up; they are special because the ordinary and mundane cracker and wine reveal the deeper reality that God is *in all* and *through all* things.

That ought to be the role of the church. Not setting itself against the world—as different from or better than—but helping its people see and experience the world as it is more deeply. What if, instead of worship existing to electrify us for the sake of the moment—a passing high to come down from as we crave the next hit—it functions more like glasses we slide on or hearing aids we power up, equipping us to better tune in to each and every moment?

Along these same lines, I'm inspired by how the late Bishop Robinson wrote of church worship: "The test of worship is how far it makes us *more sensitive* to 'the beyond in our midst,' to the Christ in the hungry, the naked, the homeless, and the prisoner. Only if we are *more likely* to recognize him there after attending an act of worship is that worship Christian rather than a piece of religiosity in Christian dress."[3]

Maybe if more churches saw their purpose this way—revealers of the Divine rather than keepers or distributors of it—we'd witness a reversal of the current exodus from most faith communities.

CHURCH WOUNDS AND TRAUMA TRIGGERS

I believe the local church still merits investing in, which is why my wife and I cofounded and copastor Sojourn Grace Collective. I do not see it, as a friend of mine says, like we are merely rearranging the chairs on the deck of the *Titanic*. That being said, before advocating why I believe people should reconsider ditching church, I think we first need permission to feel anger toward the church for how it has let us down, as well as freedom to name the betrayal of an institution conceived to heal the wounded, not create them.

---

3 John A. T. Robinson, *Honest to God* (Louisville: Westminster John Knox, 2018), 90.

Whether through sermons spewing shame and fear, spiritual leaders abusing their power, or social groups plagued by gossip and judgment, the local church possesses no shortage of trauma-inducing potential. An online community known as Exvangelical,[4] where ex-evangelicals gather for support and commiseration, reveals just how deep the pool of pain caused by the church goes. You need only scroll a few swipes before feeling entirely overwhelmed with the collective trauma held by those who've either left or were kicked out of their conservative churches.

When we experience trauma, our bodies develop a particular set of responses so that, if we sense the same sort of danger returning, our survival instincts kick in to protect us. Over time, our brains make connections between particular information and an associative emotional response. The longer our exposure to, or the deeper the intensity of, any given traumatic experience, the more ingrained the emotional response becomes. As long as our bodies carry the residue of our traumatic experiences, we remain susceptible to reexperiencing the pain of those wounds. This is known as being triggered.

The concept of a trigger has reached somewhat of a cultural fever pitch. Its massive overuse threatens to strip the word of its power, as it feels like anything nowadays could be a trigger for someone. But the term still offers massive value, so I deliberately use it here to articulate the very real experiences of many progressive Christians. If you've been one of those brave souls who's been wounded by the church and yet ventured to try a faith community again, you likely relate to the experience of getting triggered at church.

A trigger, often subtle and difficult to anticipate, can be any stimulus that prompts a recall of a previous traumatic experience.

---

4 Blake Chastain, #Exvangelical, www.exvangelicalpodcast.com.

Anything that provokes fear or brings distressing memories to the surface—such as sights, sounds, smells, sensations—can be identified as a trigger. For individuals who've suffered psychological, emotional, spiritual, sexual, or physical abuse within religious contexts, any run-of-the-mill church service could provide all sorts of potential triggers.

I once had a phone call with someone from our church whose conscious mind loved the sermon I gave one Sunday about grace. But later, as she reflected on it, she noticed how every time I said "grace," her body had a physiological reaction against it: a racing heart, increased blood pressure, and that sickly feeling in the stomach when something feels off. Another person once described how every time I put a Bible verse on the screen and read it aloud, they would clam up and devise a reason to excuse themselves. We often edit song lyrics to more closely resemble our church's values, but occasionally we leave in words such as "sinner" and "blood," and inevitably we'll hear from people who get snapped out of the moment by such terms and have a hard time reengaging. People can be triggered by activities as benign as hearing a male preacher, seeing religious icons, or being asked to pray. The point is not the trigger itself, but the pain the trigger triggers.

Truly, when considering all the ways the church has harmed people and how easy it is to be reminded of those experiences, I'm amazed at how many continue to show up. I often welcome people at Sojourn by saying, "If this is your first time with us, I want you to know just how brave you are. It took a lot of courage for you to try church again, and we see that courage and applaud you for it."

HEALING FROM RELIGIOUS PAIN

Part of the work progressive faith communities need to engage in involves understanding the painful past experiences of those in their pews. We obviously cannot avoid triggering people altogether ("One person's trigger is another person's treasure"—is that how it goes?), but we can and should bring to our gatherings a sensitivity to how our songs, prayers, and liturgy might land with people. On the flip side, those seeking to rebuild spiritual community while carrying immense church baggage should be empowered to take agency in their healing as well. I've heard it said that triggers can be signs pointing to areas of life where we haven't yet healed, and that's certainly been the case for me. If the church does its job of creating safe, non-judgmental spaces, and individuals continue to show up even when it's hard, I suspect that faith communities might be one of the best places for many of us to heal from our spiritual wounds.

Talk therapy works because you sit in a safe environment, free from judgment, where you can retell (and in a sense, relive) traumatic stories and receive new and different reactions in response. In those moments, when we receive different emotional responses to our traumatic experiences, the brain fires off neurons that create new pathways and essentially rewires itself. My therapist calls this recording over old tapes. Though it takes time—especially the deeper and longer those old tapes have been running—it can be done. With our updated pathways, we begin to have new and different emotional responses when our trauma is triggered. The important part, though, is that it happens as a result of leaning into the pain, facing the trauma, and doing so in the context of a safe and loving environment.

Recovering from spiritual trauma might very well include a similar process of recording new church tapes to overwrite the old ones, and perhaps this happens best within religious contexts. My wife and I discovered this a couple years back when we ran a small group in our living room called When Church Hurts, designed to walk people through a process for finding healing from spiritual wounds. Many of those in the group reported how important it was for them to do that work in the context of a church small group and with their pastors. Talking to their therapists about their pain, for example, of being publicly shamed in high school by their youth pastor is one thing. And it's good and important. But sharing those same stories in the company of fellow churchgoers and pastors gave them the opportunity to receive new emotional responses for their brains to begin connecting with their old stories.

Many people I've encountered over the years avoid church altogether because it's too triggering. While this certainly makes sense (and at times I've even counseled people toward a season of church abstinence), I fear they might be delaying or stunting potential healing. No doubt trauma triggers can be painful, hence the rise in trigger warnings—a brief statement preceding content (such as articles, interviews, and now even college courses), designed to caution that potentially triggering topics lay ahead. However, when it comes to PTSD, for example, research suggests that avoiding triggers reinforces the PTSD, and that systematic exposure to triggers and the memories they produce is actually the most effective path toward recovery.[5] By confronting our triggers in a safe environment, our fears subside, enabling us to move through the trauma rather than feed it. Furthermore, the longer we identify with our trauma and the more central we make it to our identity, the greater the intensity and duration of effects such as PTSD.[6] Continuing to see ourselves as victims of spiritual trauma

---

5 *Treatment of Posttraumatic Stress Disorder: An Assessment of the Evidence* (Washington, DC: National Academies Press, 2008).

6 Donald J. Robinaugh and Richard J. McNally, "Trauma Centrality and PTSD Symptom Severity in Adult Survivors of Childhood Sexual Abuse," *Journal of Traumatic Stress* 24, no. 4 (2011), doi:10.1002/jts.20656.

runs the risk of freezing our progress and distorting our identities. The goal is to move through the pain and get to a point where we see what happened to us as simply that, a thing that happened to us, not a synonym for who we are.

In no way do I advocate that a person who's experienced real harm as a result of religious leaders, institutions, or beliefs should expect—or even attempt—to find healing simply by continuing to go to church. Not at all. Rather, I believe in a comprehensive approach that very well might include a therapist and/or a spiritual director and/or medication, in addition to considering how new experiences in a safer church community can play a significant role in our healing.

SEVEN TIPS FOR TRYING CHURCH AGAIN

Humans evolved with software that drives us toward community, toward those who think, look, and act like us. We want to be part of a larger group; in fact, our bodies need it. Over time, the benefits (economically, socially, politically, etc.) to belonging in a larger group add up.[7] That means efforts to transcend communal boundaries and create spaces where diverse populations can coexist face inherent disadvantages compared to those who cater to the stay-within-the-bounds-of-our-group predispositions of our evolutionary ancestors. This explains, in part, why the largest and most "successful" (a problematic term in this context, but just go with it) churches are conservative in their theology and practice. They are organized around two of the strongest communal binding agents: shared belief and common enemies. Progressive Christian churches, on the other hand, attempt to create communities that refuse to rally around

---

7 I came across these ideas through the research of evolutionary biologist Bret Weinstein. I recommend searching his name wherever you get your podcasts and check out the many interviews he's given. Two of my favorites were on *Armchair Expert* with Dax Shepard and *Making Sense* with Sam Harris.

common enemies, and that attempt to hold space for a great diversity of belief. Our path, then, becomes exponentially more challenging.

I share this with you in part because my wife and I have spent the past half-decade swimming upstream against evolution in this way. We often look at each other and say, "This would be so much easier if we were building a conservative evangelical church!" So, if you're already part of a progressive church or if you're on the search, please be aware of just how hard it is. Now, I believe it's worth it, for I believe the potential gains and the upside are worth the struggle. But there's no denying that in communities like Sojourn Grace we forgo many of the advantages available to those who go with the flow of nature's MO.

That being said, whether you've already found a new faith community or you're open to trying church again, I have a few suggestions for the road ahead. Each one attempts to distill some of the hard-earned lessons I've acquired over the years. Some of it comes from "Colby the pastor" as I've tried to launch and lead a progressive church. Some of it comes from "Colby the fellow human" as I've tried to rediscover for myself how to do life with others. I hope they help light the way for you as they have for me.

1. SUPPORT AN INCLUSIVE CHURCH. I realize this might severely limit your pool of potential churches, but my number-one hope is that all churchgoing people who identify as Christian would attend (or at least support) inclusive churches. By this I mean the church meets the following three criteria: they are open and affirming of LGBTQ people, egalitarian in their view of women and men, and are both aware of and actively working toward dismantling systemic white supremacy. If you are inclusive in your theology but your church isn't, I think you should leave. Inclusion is an issue of justice, and it matters. Imagine you're alive in 1860 and you one day evolve to believe that owning black people as slaves is morally reprehensible, but you attend a church where the pastor owns six and his fellowship hall holds the occasional lynching rally. Of course you'd leave. With over 150 years hindsight, it's absurd to think otherwise. Hopefully, by the year 2060, these three areas of injustice will seem as obviously egregious as we now view slavery. Therefore, we need to stop supporting churches *today* that support the dehumanization of LGBTQ people, women, and and those who do not identify as white.

2. SHOW UP. Once you've identified a church you can call home, commit to showing up. I know it's hard. I know how lovely that season felt when you just got to sleep in on Sundays or drive to the mountains (okay, wait, that *does* sound pretty amazing). But change comes through movements, and movements require critical mass. Never underestimate the power of your presence. It encourages the leaders to keep on fighting, and it shows your community that you believe in what you're doing. I sympathize with the person who truly thinks they don't need to be there, but you bring an energy only *you* can bring, and without you we feel the lack. Plus, how else would you reasonably expect to build new relationships? I have a special spot on my wall where I gently bang my head every time a person tells me "I just don't feel connected" when they only show up once every four weeks.

3. BRING YOUR WHOLE SELF. Part of what made community in our previous contexts challenging stemmed from a fear of showing up authentically in our true humanity. Whether we felt we had to hide our doubts, weird beliefs, or areas of struggle, eventually we felt dis-integrated. We grew accustomed to hacking off parts of ourselves in order to fit in. Genuine connection, however, occurs not by fitting in but through a sense of belonging. Belonging says you are welcome here just as you. Fitting in says you should lose this or be more like that. You won't do anyone any favors (especially yourself) if you're still playing the old games of trying to fit in. Bring your whole self, warts and all, because in the family of God, everyone belongs.

4. SUPPORT FINANCIALLY. The complaint bucket overflows when it comes to church and money. I know how gross it can get when religious organizations and leaders leverage guilt, fear, or promises of prosperity in order to manipulate donors. That being said, let's not give money more power than it deserves. It is simply the transaction system that our societies have organized around, a basic resource for getting stuff done. Yes, you have legitimate reasons to pause before giving one more cent to another church. However, you also have the power not to let those reasons control you. If you call a church home and you're receiving some benefit from it, and/or if you support its mission and what it's trying to do and be in the world, consider doing what you can to ensure it has the resources to be as effective as possible. Every progressive Christian church I know right now is barely hanging on because of funding. When you remove motivators such as "God expects good Christians to give," it's harder to raise money. For many people who've made the Shift, it feels too vulnerable to give money to a church, because our wallets are often the last line of defense in keeping a safe distance between us and getting hurt again. We tell ourselves that if we don't invest financially, then it won't hurt as bad if the whole thing ends in disaster again. How beautiful an opportunity, then, to choose the more courageous path.

5. SKIP OCCASIONALLY. Yes, I'm contradicting #2, but let me explain. Most of us were taught that God was terribly disappointed when we failed to read the Bible enough, pray enough, or go to church enough. We constantly hustled for our worthiness, believing God was pleased when we did good religious things and bummed when we didn't. Though many of you have likely pulled out those weeds from the garden of your beliefs, they can leave behind yucky residual effects that are harder to shake. From time to time, take a break, if for no other reason than to practice being okay with not doing some of the things forced upon you by your previous religious communities.

6. EXPECT CONFLICT. I'm embarrassed to admit it, but as we started Sojourn, I was under the impression that if we did things differently, if we had better values informing how we operated, if we elevated peacemaking and mercy over rules and religiosity, then we'd be free of many of the trappings that befall other churches. Five years in, I'm still picking the crow out of my teeth. I think our community moves through conflict as healthily as we can thanks to how our values of honesty and vulnerability created a beautiful culture of grace, but people are still people. Disagreements still happen. Feelings still get hurt. Misunderstandings abound. And there will always be people who leave churches for one reason or another. Saying things like "No church is perfect" or "You can't meet everyone's expectations" is easy. But actually living it out, hanging in there when your church does finally let you down, is surprisingly hard. As best as you can, go in eyes open, understanding that better theology does not equal immunity from conflict. Decide up front that when your turn with conflict arises, you won't take the easy path of walking away.

7. PREPARE FOR DIVERSITY. Similar to the previous point, you have to learn to hold space for diversity if you're going to thrive in any community. This feels especially true in progressive circles. Most of our previous churches built unity through shared beliefs and common enemies. These can be powerful binding agents, but as mentioned, most progressive Christian churches aren't built around such convictions. As such, you'll find yourself doing life with people who think very differently from you on all sorts of issues. Try and focus on what you hold in common, such as a shared commitment to justice, a conviction that love matters more than belief, and a desire to learn from others so that you can always be growing. It can feel a little clunky, that first small group with a Buddhist, an agnostic, and a throuple[8], but hang in there, hold things loosely, and enjoy how much you'll grow.

Those of us wounded by religion have built walls high around our hearts, and for good reasons. The walls have a one-way mirror so we can look out, but don't dare try to look in. Walls like this end up blocking everything. We think we're only restricting the potential for pain and betrayal—who wants to experience that again? But we can't selectively block out some emotions and not others. The wall will also prevent joy, connection, and love.

May we find the courage to let down our walls, open up to one another, and discover how the narrow path of vulnerability and trust can lead us to a more connected and thriving life.

Even if that means trying church again.

---

8 A three-way relationship. It's like a couple, but with three.

8

Waging the War Within

What to Do When Your Old Self Sabotages Your Efforts to Grow

Head sagging and frozen in malaise, though I couldn't muster the energy to confirm it, I knew she sat there staring at the top of my head like a cat over a gopher hole. Sitting as far as I could on the right side of her baby blue love seat with my legs extra crossed, I absentmindedly spun my wedding ring around my finger—a dead giveaway for my grave discomfort. Neither my body nor my mind intended to open up.

I wouldn't call it an aggressive stare, as in, *I've asked the question, now it's your turn to answer.* No, I sat on the receiving end of the maddeningly patient passivity of a therapist trained in Emotionally Focused Therapy (EFT). She could out-wait even the most skilled in the art of sustaining awkward silence (which I've always considered a decent skill of mine, but I'm clearly the Padawan here). An unassuming candle in the corner coated the room with a hint of lavender, clinically proven to soothe. A white noise machine hummed somewhere unseen, coaxing me to relax. None of it worked. Worse, I knew my therapist would sit there, as long as it took, committed to not breaking the silence until I responded.

At that point I had been in therapy for about ten months, a decent-sized miracle, really. For years my wife suggested I talk to a counselor, and for years I deflected. Partially because within the conservative Christianity of my youth brews a mistrust of the therapeutic world. It's suggested—or even outright taught—that prayer and Bible study provide sufficient means for repairing breaches of the heart and mind, thereby creating ample shame for those who consider going outside the church for help.

The other reason I resisted therapy? It terrified me. I expend a great deal of energy projecting an image that I have it all together, that I have no real problems, that I'm not human like the rest of you. Why would I willingly put myself at the mercy of someone who would see right through my well-rehearsed act? I'd rather chew broken glass.

And there you have it: shame and fear, possibly the two most powerful forces keeping us from living a thriving, abundant life. They serve as the primary weapons in the internal battles when one part of us says yes to the Spirit's invitation to grow, but another part—which I'll call the old self—immediately resists. The old self, it turns out, has a particular attachment to who we've become. A vested interest, you might say. It worked hard to get us here and sees no sense in changing now, so it pulls out all the stops to sabotage our transformation, leveraging shame and fear at every turn in its efforts to prevent a new self from emerging.

Perhaps the deepest, most personal obstacle we'll face on our journey toward becoming a progressive Christian is this struggle between our old and new selves. Eventually, we'll need to address whatever hostilities or misgivings emerge with our family, friends, or former church community, but first we must wage the war within. Our old selves, carefully fashioned through years of Sunday school lessons, Bible studies, and potlucks, will not easily relent to these newfangled ideas that beckon us onward.

A tale of two brothers found in Genesis 32 illustrates what can happen when we perch on the precipice of breaking through to a whole new way of seeing both ourselves and the world around us.

A LONG-ANTICIPATED REUNION

As you may recall from the flannelgraph, the brotherly relationship between Jacob and Esau ended abruptly when Jacob—for the second time—bamboozled his older brother out of his rightful blessing and inheritance. Jacob fled home when his mom warned him of Esau's fury and intention for murderous revenge. So, with thievery on one side and death threats on the other, the brothers hadn't seen each other in twenty years by time we get to Jacob devising a plan to return home in Genesis 32.

Decades had past, and now Jacob, the clear antagonist in the sibling rivalry, dared to hope his brother would consider reconciliation. While still a ways off from Esau's land, Jacob sent messengers ahead to inform his brother that he, Jacob, had become a wealthy man and was returning home, hopeful that Esau had spent the last twenty years cooling down. The messengers returned and reported to Jacob, "We went out to your brother Esau, and he's coming to meet you with four hundred men" (Gen 32:6). This was no welcome party. Four hundred men meant an army. Esau intended to fight. If revenge is best served cold, this one had been on ice for two decades.

Jacob, terrified at the potential bloodbath awaiting him, quickly split up his camp so as to minimize his losses if his brother indeed attacked. Before the sun went down, Jacob concocted a plan he hoped would pacify his brother and keep himself off the tip of Esau's spear. From his vast wealth of livestock, Jacob put together a bountiful gift of goats, rams, camels, and more (history's first Edible Arrangement). He split up the gift into three separate groups and gave them the following instructions:

> Go ahead of me and put some distance between each of the herds . . .
> When my brother Esau meets you and asks you, "Who are you with?
> Where are you going? And whose herds are these in front of you?," say,
> "They are your servant Jacob's, a gift sent to my master Esau. And Jacob
> is actually right behind us" (vv. 16–18).

However, Jacob *wouldn't* be right behind. Rather, another round of gifts would follow. Three times Jacob scheduled this charade, each time insisting, "Your servant Jacob is right behind us." With this plan, "Jacob thought, I may be able to pacify Esau with the gift I'm sending ahead. When I meet him, perhaps he will be kind to me" (v. 20).

It's embarrassing to admit, but as I read Jacob's plan, I find myself nodding along and thinking, "Not a bad idea. That might work!" I've got some Jacob in me, and this plan feels familiar to ones I've concocted in the past. I can't count the number of times in my relationship with Kate when I messed up or wounded her in some way and, instead of owning it and saying, "I was wrong and I am sorry," I found myself doing all these little tricks to try to smooth things over. To try, as Jacob put it, to pacify my wife. I did extra laundry, cleaned the garage, sent a sweet text, or basically anything other than acknowledging that I messed up.

Jacob might have feared his brother and what he would do, but he seemed equally terrified to admit his own failure. Afraid to admit that he wronged Esau all those years ago. And so, in his fear, he hoped some sheep, donkeys, and goats would distract his brother enough so that the hard conversation never happened. Jacob feared admitting—to both himself and to Esau—that he royally screwed up.

Jacob's desire to reconnect with Esau? A good thing! Jacob's effort to sidestep his responsibility in their fracturing? Not so good. Keep this in mind as we read what happens next in the story, when out of nowhere, Jacob finds himself in a fight for his life.

LATE-NIGHT WRESTLING MATCH

I've never been in a real fight. As an aspiring pacifist, I'm hopeful to keep my streak intact, but if it ever happened, I'm assuming that— unless the odds stacked heavily in my favor—I'd lose miserably. My arms and legs are sticks, nary a muscle with which to inflict damage. And my hands? Well, they're accustomed to the more refined, precise motions of typing, drawing cartoons, and playing guitar. Me throwing a punch would be like the time I visited a museum in San Francisco and drank from a toilet that had been converted into a drinking fountain. Sure, you could do it, but everyone watching will cringe at the awkwardness of it all.

That being said, I've rehearsed being in a fight plenty of times in my mind, just in case. With Jason Bourne scenes running through my head, a tiny part of me imagines that maybe I could parry my opponent's blows, surprising both them *and* me. (Those who know me best are laughing right now. Feel free to join them.) With four hundred men marching his way, I'm assuming Jacob prepared himself just in case his plan failed, perhaps rehearsing fighting techniques in his head too. However, no doubt he awoke unprepared for the fight that actually did take place that night.

Before going to sleep, the storyteller says Jacob took his family across the Jabbok River and into Esau's territory. Jacob then returned back over the river to spend the night alone. Stressed and weary from the day's efforts, and anxious about what awaited him, Jacob went to bed that night isolated from his family, perhaps searching for some calm before the storm. There, in his loneliness and fear, the storyteller says, "a man wrestled with him until dawn broke" (Gen 32:24). The man's identity stays hidden, and we never learn where he came from or why he showed up ready to rumble. We simply go from Jacob sleeping by himself across the Jabbok River to a sudden and intense all-night wrestling match.

The mystery man eventually realized he couldn't win. So, with dawn breaking (v. 24) and his defeat imminent, the man pulled out one last cheap shot and tore a muscle in Jacob's thigh (v. 25). Finally, the man requested to be set free, but Jacob bizarrely replied with, "I won't let you go until you bless me" (v. 26). The nearly defeated stranger saw Jacob's question and rose with one of his own, "What's your name?"

Quite the bizarre story, isn't it? A stranger comes out of nowhere, picks a fight with Jacob, nearly loses before taking a cheap shot, then gets asked for a blessing *by the very guy he's wrestling*, and caps it all off by inquiring, "What's your name?" His question, at first glance, suggests that the mystery man didn't know Jacob's identity. But a deeper reading, and my intuition, leads me to believe there's something else going on here.

THE BATTLE WITHIN

When the mystery man asked for his name, Jacob told him. But then the man said, "Your name won't be Jacob any longer, but Israel." A common storytelling technique in the Bible, name changes signify a shift or evolution of the character.[1] Jacob went into this epic all-nighter as Jacob, but he came out of it as Israel, which literally means in Hebrew "God shall fight." Instead of always fighting and

---

1 E.g., Abram and Sarai to Abraham and Sarah. Simon to Peter. Saul to Paul.

scheming for the outcome he desired, Jacob's new name indicates a shift in perspective: he is now willing to let God do the fighting. Instead of grabbing and controlling, Jacob's new identity as Israel would be about letting go and serving. What an incredible illustration of the journey of faith—particularly the kind that many of us undergo as we become progressive Christians.

Tradition suggests that this late-night rendezvous involved Jacob wrestling either God or an angel. I don't find either of those readings particularly compelling. I'm not saying they're wrong, or that people haven't found inspiration or deep meaning from such readings. But when I read this story, I sense Jacob is wrestling with *himself*. Or, more precisely, with his old self. Which would help explain why, when Jacob responds with the same question, of "What is *your* name?," the mystery man asks, "Why do you ask for *my* name?" (v. 29). Almost as if to say, "Why are you asking? You already know who I am. You already know my name, because I am you."

Jacob's wrestling story serves as an archetype for approaching the threshold of deeply personal transformation. Of charting a new course for who we are becoming. It illustrates the struggle we face when our old self is asked to make way for our newer, more expansive self. Jacob had been accustomed to a certain way of life, one that involved deception and manipulation. One that involved patterns of running away from conflict and not taking responsibility for his actions. Then, in the middle of the night, he received the gift of seeing his old self in a new light. The intense wrestling match revealed an invitation to transformation's threshold, a caterpillar making its first effort to break through the cocoon.

I faced a similar internal battle as I sat on my therapist's baby blue couch, anxiously spinning my wedding ring. We had just been talking about how I felt like I couldn't be the man my wife needed me to be. The man my wife *deserved* that I be. She needed me to show up to our relationship in ways I didn't know how to do. Including things like taking responsibility for my actions when I wounded her, not shutting down and shutting her out when I got upset, and being honest enough to name my feelings instead of passive-aggressively punishing her through body language and gaslighting. I had developed these patterns of behavior over the previous three decades, most of them passed on to me by my own family (much like Jacob, whose mother helped him manipulate and deceive his father in Gen 27:5–13). For me to begin to change, to fully confront all these behaviors that had for so long defined Colby, felt like an insurmountable task.

I remember adamantly telling Kate in the midst of one of our fights, "I can't do it. I just *can't*. I can't be the person you need me to be. It's too hard."

When I shared those words with my therapist, she calmly but sternly said, "Colby, I want you to consider reframing that. I think it's not that it's too hard for you. I think it's too scary for you." I resented her already. She went on, "It's not so much that you *can't* do it, but that you're *afraid* to."

FEAR STARTS AND STOPS WITH ME

Her words plowed uninvited into my gut, as truth has a way of doing. Still, I resisted, terrified to face the idea of becoming a new person. It felt safer (easier?) to keep my potential new self in the category of things that are too hard. If that's the case, if it's just too difficult for me, then I could hardly be blamed for my inability to become a more empathetic, communicative, present spouse. I could shrug my emotionally dead shoulders and say, "Whelp, sorry, but I tried. As it turns out, it's just slightly beyond my ability." That option gave me an out. I could avoid transformation *and* avoid being responsible for it. Like, sure, I could *try* to become an

NBA player, but when I fail, you can't seriously blame *me* for it. It's clearly outside my capacity.

But moving it into the fear category? Crap. What excuse did I have then? I'm horribly afraid of rats, but if I absolutely had to be in the same room as one, or had to hold one (God forbid! I die at the thought), I could do it. Ability isn't holding me back—it's fear, which starts and stops with me.

My fear kept me from even trying to be the man my wife needed me to be. Yet, at the same time, moving from a place of "I can't do it" to "I'm afraid to do it" suddenly liberated me to see entirely new possibilities. Scary though it was, because I knew it was just fear that was holding me back, I also knew I could master that fear. I've done scary things before. Impossible things might always remain so, but scary things can be overcome.

I went into my therapist's office that afternoon as Colby, but I left as—well, I guess my name is still Colby, but you get my point. A radical transformation took place inside me, and when I finally uncrossed my legs, stopped spinning my ring, and let myself open up, my journey toward a new self began—unburdened by the lie that I couldn't change and empowered to face my fears and grow.

I'm still on the journey, obviously, but I'm much more likely to do what I couldn't—or rather, wouldn't—do. Such as sit in my own discomfort and name my feelings honestly so that my wife doesn't have to guess. Or stay in the room and remain present when we are fighting instead of retreating and shutting down. I am choosing a new way to engage with conflict, and it starts with my willingness to name when and how I've messed up, and to stay with the conflict until peace can be found. While not solving all the problems, this new (and for me, very different) approach to conflict provides me and Kate a fighting chance for a healthy and happy relationship. I'm slowly laying the old me to rest, believing the Christ pattern offers hope for a newer, less fear-filled me.

When I consider the intense, overwhelming battle that waged within me—both in my therapist's office and the years leading up to it—describing it as a wrestling match with myself sounds about right. I identify with Jacob and empathize with his desire to avoid owning his mistakes, perhaps explaining why I see the mysterious figure as an alter ego Jacob instead of God or an angel.

And I haven't even gotten to the best part of the story yet.

FROM BRIBERY TO BOWING

The rising sun roused Jacob, now Israel, but before he broke camp to rejoin his family, he named the place "Peniel, because I've seen God face-to-face, and my life has been saved" (Gen 32:30). I assume this is an expression, because "no one has seen the face of God and lived" to tell about it (Exod 33:20). When Jacob says his life has been saved, this word can also be translated as *delivered* or *rescued*. Both words aptly describe emerging victorious after battling your old self. But even more beautiful, this word in Hebrew is *natsal*, which literally means "to snatch away." In his all-night wrestling match, Old Jacob got snatched away and replaced with Jacob 2.0, a.k.a. Israel.

Watch what happens next. Not only does the story end beautifully, but it also reveals a vision of true transformation:

> Jacob looked up and saw Esau approaching with four hundred men.
> Jacob divided the children among Leah, Rachel, and the two women
> servants. He put the servants and their children first, Leah and her
> children after them, and Rachel and Joseph last. He himself went
> in front of them and bowed to the ground seven times as he was
> approaching his brother. (Gen 33:1–3)

Did you catch it? Recall that Jacob's original plan involved waves of bribery sent on ahead while he cowardly waited in the rear, hoping to pacify Esau through a lavish gift parade. But now, on day one of Jacob 2.0, as he saw his brother and four hundred men approaching, Jacob marched out first. He led the way. And instead of making excuses or trying to sweet-talk his way into his brother's good graces, he humbly bowed to the ground seven times in full deference and respect to his brother.

With his days of deceit and manipulation behind him, Jacob approached his brother fully trusting that God shall fight ("Israel"). For me, this is about taking a posture of openness and vulnerability. When we learn to accept ourselves just as we are, such self-love renders us undefended in the face of conflict. We no longer need to fight to be seen, strive to be valued, or hustle for our worth. Jacob laid down the weapons he used for so long in his efforts to keep himself alive, and realized his best bet moving forward was to *let go and let God*. (Sorry! I know that probably made you cringe, I felt it too. But there's a layer of truth in that old saying that I find helpful, especially in this context.)

Jacob let go of his constant efforts to control and deceive, and in its place he allowed his acceptance as a loved child of God do the "fighting" for him. A changed man, indeed. The old self had gone away (*natsal*) and the new had come.

WINNING THE BATTLE WITHIN

As you move from conservative to progressive Christianity, one of the first battles you'll encounter is the one within. Your old self has, for years, developed ideas and beliefs about who you are, who God is, and how you fit within your religious community. An identity has been built, and evolving beyond that identity threatens the "you" who got you there. Your old self panics as fear and shame come online and need to be acknowledged, addressed, and eventually overcome. You'll have plenty more challenges ahead, and it's best to face those challenges with eyes wide open to the ways fear and shame can creep in and sabotage your efforts to grow.

It's scary to change, grow, and transform. Believe me, I know. Yet, I invite you to stare fear right in its ugly face and say, "Thank you for how you've helped get me here and shaped the person I am today. You've served me well in the past. But now you're holding me back from who I want to become." Like Jacob, we must reject the impulse to hold on tight and try to control; instead, we must seek to open up, trust, and let go. As you lay down the weapons you once used to defend yourself, may you embody Israel ("God shall fight!") and discover all the armor you need resting in the truth that you are a loved child of God.

Likewise, shame wants you to believe that you can't do it. That you don't have what it takes. That you'll never survive out there, alone, detached from your old faith communities. Shame wants you to turn around and go back home, believing you are unworthy of love and belonging. It wants you to ignore the deep cries within your soul, the ones begging you to spread your wings and fly. But bring the shame into the light! Do not try to outrun or hide your fears, flaws, and frustrations. Many of us left conservative Christianity because of the lack of space for doubts and questions. You had to be perfect, and shame thrives in those conditions. Your new self, however, doesn't tolerate the hiding or pretending. The more we talk about the things that trouble us, and the more we name our struggles and bring them to the light, the less power shame has.

Jacob faced his fears, fought against his old impulses, and showed up the next day in a whole new way. His brother's response says it all: "But Esau ran to meet him, threw his arms around his neck, kissed him, and they wept" (Gen 33:4). We may not always get such storybook endings, but overcoming fear and shame will at least create pathways for a life filled with joy, peace, and love, whereas the roads of fear and shame will only ever end in separation, isolation, and death.

There is one final detail from this story that I've omitted until now. After Jacob wrestled and overcame his old self, the storyteller says, "The sun rose as Jacob passed Penuel, *limping because of his thigh*" (Gen 32:32, emphasis mine). Here's the thing: we don't wage the war within and come out unscathed. The person who has emerged victorious, overcoming the fear and shame that rise up when we undergo personal transformation, will forever be altered by the deep changes within. They will walk with a limp, evidence of their courageous journey of transformation.

For years, I had no hitch in my giddy-up. My gait was smooth, like the unbroken surface of a just-opened jar of peanut butter. But rather than a sign of my awesomeness (as I deluded myself to believe), it indicated how I had not yet traveled the path of Jacob on the banks of the Jabbok River. I had not yet embarked on the journey of the warrior, as Pema Chodron says in *When Things Fall Apart*, and sat in my hot loneliness long enough to face who I had become—a necessary step to begin the process of becoming who I truly long to be.

For me, that looked like fighting my fears and going to therapy—where I'd continue to face them again and again—and watch as the layers of shame I carried slowly fell away. For Jacob, it looked like humbling himself to his brother, whom he'd wronged so many years before, and throwing himself upon his mercy. No longer running from his failures, but owning them and choosing honesty over fear and deception.

Whether you're just beginning your journey toward progressive Christianity or you've been on the road for a while, we all must face those moments when we battle against an older version of our selves who resents growth. When those days come, may you remember that fear and shame don't stand a chance against love and trust. Your new, more expansive and inclusive self is wholly loved by God just as you are. And may you discover a trust that the God who brought you up to this point has not and will not abandon you now. Like a parent over their child, God cheers you on as you grow.

When the dust settles and the sun rises, when the new day begins, when the old self stays buried in the ground while the new you rises triumphantly, don't be surprised if you walk a bit slower, a bit more crookedly.

This doesn't mean you're doing it wrong. The limp is the sign that you're ready for the journey ahead.

Relax,
You've Come So Far

What to Do When You're Mortified by Your Past Beliefs and Behavior

I once scared the hell out of ninety-five high school students. Don't worry, my boss loved it.

It happened at an event called Boycott Hell Night—held annually on Halloween—and my particular moment of fame came on its third anniversary. That year boasted a record turnout with over four hundred high school students showing up to a youth group event instead of, you know, doing something secular like trick-or-treating. I had been an intern at the church for over a year and had just started my sophomore year in college when my boss, the youth pastor, handed over the prestigious role of presenting the Boycott Hell message. It was a veritable dream come true.

My job: deliver a twenty-minute talk about hell, drudging up the scariest and hottest images I could imagine and employing the most manipulative techniques at my disposal. Like this (which I actually said out loud in a room full of human beings): "Imagine one night you and your friend are driving home from a party and you get into a car accident and both die. You're a Christian, but you've never talked to your friend about Jesus. At the gates of heaven, Saint Peter lets you through but calls a demon to take your friend away, and they'll spend eternity in hell. As your friend is dragged by the demon over the coals and toward the darkness, he turns back and screams, 'Why didn't you ever tell me?'"

My goal was to convince as many students as possible to accept Jesus into their hearts and thus save them from the aforementioned fires of hell. When my message concluded, if you combined the number of hands raised during the closing prayer with the number of cards turned in where the box "I got saved!" was checked, ninety-five students changed their eternal destiny that night.

I went home proud as a dove (like a peacock, but more spiritual). My peers and professors the next day endured no shortage of humble-bragging as I touted my 1-in-4 conversion ratio. Billy Graham had better watch his six.

INSUFFERABLE AND OVERSAVED

An insufferable Christian from ages seventeen to twenty-seven, I'm embarrassed when I think back to moments like Boycott Hell Night. I refer to those days as being "oversaved," a term I learned years ago that most readers won't need explained. During that decade of my life, no conversation with me was safe. I could spin any topic into a segue about salvation.

For example, I'd sit at Starbucks and glance across the shop to see two people minding their own business while enjoying an over-roasted coffee. In my mind I would swear I heard the voice of God (perhaps not audibly, but in a way that I still described as "God told me") prompting me to pester these innocent strangers about why they needed to know Jesus as their personal lord and savior. I did this regularly.

At restaurants, my friends cringed when the waiter came to take our order because they knew what came next. I had this routine where, once I'd politely introduced myself and said, "I'll have the bacon cheeseburger, no pickles, and an ice water—hold the ice," I would follow up with, "Before you leave, I'd love to ask, is there anything I can pray for you about?" Now, to be fair, this question occasionally sparked a wonderful conversation where the server genuinely felt seen and loved, so it wasn't the worst habit of my oversaved days. Yet, you can imagine how often my inquiry was met with eye rolls, polite annoyance, or back-of-kitchen mockery. To make matters worse, I would often leave my tip rolled up in a gospel tract, you know, just in case Daphne wanted to spend her smoke break traveling down the Romans Road.

Whether warning teenagers about the darkness and suffering awaiting their stubborn hearts, interrupting latte sippers to interrogate the status of their souls, or spinning a conversation about "Scrambled or sunny-side up?" to "Are you frazzled and want to give up?", I never missed an opportunity to offer my gift of evangelism gratis.

As I look back on that season of my life, even more than the unsolicited proselytization or manipulative sermons, I deeply regret the general energy I exuded to my non-Christian family and friends. I couldn't just relax in their presence, and I'm certain they felt it. They knew I believed deep in my bones that unless they accepted Jesus as their lord and savior, then the great beyond held torment for them. Even when I kept my mini sermons and Jesus jukes at bay,

I still carried a general air of disappointment around people who didn't share my beliefs.

It grieves me to think of how my self-righteous surety cast myriad judgy shadows on folks in my orbit. Waitresses didn't need my gospel tract or spiritualized solicitations; they needed a good tip and a kind patron. Strangers at Starbucks didn't need interrupting and inquisitions; they needed to be left alone. And my friends didn't need my judgmental asides or pious attitude; they needed just another kid like them who was stumbling along, trying to figure life out, and who was there if they needed something.

Like Ebenezer Scrooge waking up from the longest sleep of his life, I am ashamed when I think back to how I thought about and treated people.

I CAN'T BELIEVE I BELIEVED . . .

In the last chapter, we looked at one of the more deeply personal obstacles in becoming a progressive Christian, namely when our old self puts up a vicious fight and resists our new self's faith exploration. I've discovered that soon after the new self wins a few battles and tries on an article or two of progressive Christian clothing, another inner obstacle emerges when we experience moments of horror upon reflection of how we used to think and act while entrenched in our more conservative ways of seeing the world.

"I can't believe I used to believe that!" we tell our friends, mortified at some previous doctrine that, at the time, we held with deep conviction. Now the thought makes us cringe. The most common beliefs that cause this response include: the condemnation of LGBTQ individuals, the notion that God predestines people for hell, and the idea that women are inferior (and therefore ought to be subservient) to men. We might imagine a time machine taking us back to a Bible study where you ardently defended and masterfully articulated why science is wrong and God created the universe in six literal days. Or perhaps we dig up your journal from five years ago and it betrays earnest prayers for God to change your child's sexual orientation. Or, like me, maybe you're haunted by the memories of explaining—with a straight face—to your best friend why it "truly is loving for God to send them to hell if they don't believe in Jesus."

I remember when I thought all religions of the world (other than Christianity) were lies leading people to damnation. I remember arguing incessantly that the Bible is absolutely without error, a perfect articulation of God's heart and mind. Now, if I try to get in touch with the person who believed like that, I'm dumbfounded. I'm embarrassed that it once seemed reasonable and logical that God would order a Hitlerian genocide of an entire people group, or that Jesus would one day return with trumpet blasts and snatch the bodies of Christians just before unleashing a series of violent plagues upon the unbelieving schmucks left behind. (Even as I type those sentences, I find myself amping up the egregiousness of it all because they feel so bizarre and offensive, which leads me to describe them so it's obvious that's not what I think anymore.)

It feels impossible nowadays to connect with these old beliefs. I try to wrap my head around them, but they feel foreign and distant. It's like how you sometimes wake up from a deep sleep and for the first fifteen seconds you can vividly recall the dream you just had, but then the details get fuzzy and you barely remember a thing.

In my early post-Shift days, I could easily become paralyzed with guilt around such recollections. I was appalled that I used to think the way I did or treat people with such frivolity. Fortunately, since then, I've come to see those moments of horror and shame in a new light. I now have a framework that helps me not just make sense of my past but also better illuminates the present. Plus, I've discovered some helpful practices to make sure that in the future I don't make the same mistakes.

It starts with bacon. And babies.

FROM MILK TO MEAT

Unless you are part of the 2 percent of the population who suffers from ageusia (a condition in which you can't taste anything because your taste buds are defective), then there's little denying that bacon is the Chuck Norris of food. It goes with anything and makes everything it touches better. Even vegetarians know the beauty of bacon, though their conscience convinces them otherwise. Prometheus may have thought the fire he stole from the gods to give humanity was the gift, but the real gift is how fire eventually allowed us to cook pigs and discover bacon. Bacon is best prepared in a frying pan on the stove and I won't hear otherwise. If you come at me insisting any sort of "baking in the oven" nonsense, to quote Jesus, "Get behind me, Satan," and "forgive them Father, for they know not what they do."

I like to start with a cold pan on the stove, carefully laying down each fatty strip (none of this thin-cut tomfoolery) as the medium heat slowly works up a sizzle. Make sure the strips aren't overlapping—you want the entire surface of each strip to get its own spot against the pan, dancing cheek to cheek. Crack some ground pepper on top. Then crack some more (you should feel almost embarrassed at the amount you're lavishing). As the bacon starts to soften and scrunch, flip and pepper the other side. Don't be shy. Proceed flipping every two minutes or so until one side is deep red. One more flip to finish off the other side ought do it (probably thirty seconds max, at this point), then remove the bacon and lay your bounty flat on paper towels. Keep in mind that after it's removed from the heat, the bacon will continue cooking. Let it do its thing; it wants to be perfect for you. If you notice the bacon getting orange in the pan, you've cooked it too long. Avoid the temptation to make bacon-flavored charcoal—people who say they like it that way simply haven't had it prepared for them properly. Finally, pat down the excess grease, but not so aggressively that you soak up everything and leave it desiccated. If it looks like those small discs of watercolor paints before you've added water, ease up on your grease patting, pal. The final product should be a nice combination of crisp with a slight chew, deep red with a hint of white at the fattiest parts, with just the slightest kick thanks to your black pepper barrage.

The fact that I used four hundred words of this book to describe bacon should show you just how seriously I take it. But here's a truly tragic thing about bacon: babies (which I love almost as much as bacon) can't eat it. For starters, they lack teeth. Beyond that, their little digestive systems simply aren't developed enough to handle the fatty, salty, chewy goodness. It's one of life's best offerings, yet babies can't partake.

However, unless someone is unconscionably cruel, no one would consider mocking a baby for their inability to eat bacon. No one would laugh and point and rub it in their tiny, squishy face that they can't enjoy the food equivalent of a sunset over a Balinese beach. Obviously, mocking a baby is absurd, but you couldn't even imagine someone thinking less of a baby because they couldn't eat bacon, as though their inability indicated a lack of effort. We simply accept that these miniature humans have some growing up to do before partaking in such thick-cut slices of heaven.

In a letter he wrote to the church he started in Corinth, the apostle Paul said, "Brothers and sisters, I couldn't talk to you like spiritual people but like unspiritual people, like babies in Christ. I gave you milk to drink instead of solid food, because you weren't up to it yet" (1 Cor 3:1–2). Did you catch that? Paul said he gave them milk instead of solid food (bacon!) because they weren't up to it yet. He assessed their developmental stage and accommodated in kind. Members of the Corinthian church tangled themselves in jealousy and quarreling around which teacher they liked best, and even though Paul may have wanted to discuss more advanced ideas of how to live in the way of Jesus, he met them where they were. In this case, they were mere infants in Christ.

When I think back to my oversaved days, it's easy to get bogged down in embarrassment. But reframing that season of my life as simply one developmental stage among (hopefully) many has done wonders for my well-being. As a babe in Christ, I did the best I could with what I had. Sure, I know more now. I've moved on from some of the more primitive ideas about God and the Bible that once fueled my naive adventures. Back then I was like a first-grade kid who's mastered addition and subtraction but whose little brain would explode at the suggestion of negative or imaginary numbers. You do the best with what you have, and if you're graced to someday receive more, great! Enjoy all the fun, new, fancy tricks now at your disposal. But it doesn't do you any good to belittle past versions of yourself when, odds are, no one could reasonably expect you to have done differently.

Babies can't eat bacon. The reasonable response is not to disparage or disregard them for it. May we take the same approach when considering who we were in our more conservative Christian days.

NO OTHER OPTION

I want to push deeper here because I think this particular obstacle trips us up more than it needs to. I really believe that once we reframe our thinking, we can shed all sorts of unnecessary bad feelings around what we used to believe and how we used to treat people.

Not only does it make sense to look back at previous versions of ourselves with grace because a certain degree of development is necessary and normal, but we'd also do well to consider that maybe who we were was all we could have been. In other words, what if you legitimately had no other option than to be a self-righteous prat whose beliefs were narrow-minded and whose actions were hollow-hearted? I realize that not everyone looks back at their faith journey quite as harshly as I do, nor were they quite the self-righteous prat that I was. But that's the good news! If even I can find a way free from this obstacle, then surely you can too. Especially if it's less intense for you.

Consider the following: You didn't choose your parents. You didn't choose where you were born or when. You didn't choose what sort of home you grew up in, what religion (if any) your parents subscribed to, nor what values guided your family system. You didn't choose your earliest friends, your teachers, or your pastors. You didn't choose where you rank on the five big personality traits—which play considerable roles in what resonates with us religiously, politically, and ethically. You didn't choose your Enneagram number, hair color, height, or vision or hearing ability. You get the point.

Now, think back to some of the earliest memories that shaped your religious worldview. The prayers said over you at bedtime. The conversations your parents had with you about God. The sermons preached and the lessons taught in Sunday school. Consider how your beliefs were shaped by your friends, your personal tragedies growing up, and your parents' expectations of who you should be in the world.

All of this created the unique conditions in which your beliefs about everything formed. Outside a few variables here and there, is it too far of a stretch to consider that the person you became, the person comfortable inside conservative Christianity, is realistically the only person who could have come into being? Regardless of where you fall on the free will versus determinism spectrum, we all must acknowledge the sheer magnitude of significant factors that undeniably shaped us along the way and that without a doubt were beyond our control or choosing. With that in mind, how could we not grant our past selves enough grace to at least let us off the hook for some of who we used to be?

My brother and his family used to care for foster kids, specifically those who came from traumatic home environments. Most of the young children who showed up on their doorstep came with fetal alcohol syndrome or some other behavior-altering condition they developed as a consequence of their parents' neglect or abuse. My brother and sister-in-law were trained for such situations, and they knew they couldn't parent these kids the same way they parented their biological children. Blaming kids who come from such environments—where clearly they were unwilling participants in the chemistry and manufacturing of their psychological and biological makeup—when they fail to respond to relatively normal direction or stimulus is the height of ignorance.

Even if the scale is smaller, you are still a product of factors outside your control. So, shower yourself in kindness. When you bump up against those moments of disbelief over what you used to believe or are mortified at how you used to treat people as a result of your religious convictions, take a breath and remember that in some sense you had very little potential to be anyone else.

Before moving on, I want to make one final observation as it relates to showing ourselves kindness for our past. While I believe such self-love and self-grace are necessary for our well-being, we also must take into consideration what real harm we may have done to others as a result of our previous religious beliefs and/or political commitments. For example, if your past involves the dehumanization of LGBTQ people (especially those you know personally), the degradation of women, or the discrimination against different ethnicities, then simply letting yourself off the hook for your past ignorance may not be enough. Your future well-being may very well be contingent upon your willingness to repent of past prejudicial beliefs, coupled with efforts to set wrongs aright. What that might look like in your particular context and how to go about it is beyond the scope of this book. But if you at all feel as though you've wronged people in the past as a result of your more conservative ideas, then may you remember the ancient story from last chapter and consider how, like Jacob before his brother Esau, you might humble yourself to others, acknowledge your errors, and seek reconciliation and repair.

THE INEVITABILITY OF CHANGE

You haven't arrived. Sure, you might have deeper, more gracious ideas about the world than you used to. You might have a broader awareness of science or history or sociology. You probably feel better about your overall current state of belief (or disbelief) than when you used to run in more conservative circles. But you haven't arrived. Odds are, some of what we've covered in this chapter in terms of being embarrassed by past versions of our selves will come up again later in life as well. To prepare for that, I suggest you memorize the lessons learned in Spencer Johnson's 1998 bestselling book about business management, *Who Moved My Cheese?*

The book's core message revolves around the inevitability of change in the workplace. It offers a simple six-step process:

1. Anticipate change (assume it is normal and will occur).

2. Monitor for change (regularly check in to see what, if anything, has changed).

3. Adapt to change quickly (the quicker you can let go of the old and get on with the new, the better).

4. Actually change (reality should be markedly different at this point).

5. Enjoy change (savor the new way of things).

6. Be ready to change and enjoy again (hold it all loosely, because change is inevitable).

Channeling all my skills in what the world has demeaningly labeled "dad humor" (I think it's just called humor, but whatever), I suggest that one of the ways you can stay sane in your Shift is by remembering the principles of this book, but change the title to *Who Moved My Cheese-us?* (like *Jesus*, but cheesier. Get it?). Anticipate your continued growth and transformation. Regularly check in to see if what you currently believe lines up with a year ago. Once you've noticed a change somewhere, simply let the old belief go—because you've already come to see how faith doesn't require you to hold your beliefs tight. With openness and trust, implement your new ideas and values. Test them out in the world. If they don't yield good fruit, then let those ones go too! Enjoy the new place you're in, because why not? You're never not here, right now. Might as well enjoy it. And as you look ahead in life, remember that you still haven't arrived. One day you'll look back on what you believe now with wonder and curiosity, maybe even disbelief that you ever thought that way.

THE BLACK BELT OF GRACE

We start by appreciating the developmental nature of spiritual transformation, then zoom out further to accept that who we become (at any stage, really) remains largely beyond our control. Next, we reset our expectations for the future and assume we'll continue to change and evolve. Finally, we are ready for the black belt of grace, the master level of applying kindness with regards to the reality of faith development and transformation.

Black belt–level grace occurs when we apply all of what we've learned about ourselves in this chapter to the people we come in contact with every day. The magic of the way forward through this particular obstacle is that not only does it alleviate undue pain and suffering from our own lives, but it opens up the possibility for better connection with friends and family members who might still believe as we once did. Picture those from your previous conservative church or family and spend a moment imagining their lives. Imagine how they might have grown up. See if you can find space to accept that they might very well be doing the best they can with the cards they've been dealt. Perhaps they, for whatever reasons, still require spiritual milk as you once did.

Then consider that, just as you went on a very unique journey of spiritual transformation that included all sorts of surprising twists and turns, perhaps they too might one day change. Even if they don't (because, honestly, some people stay on milk forever), you will greatly help your own mental well-being by showering them with the same grace you give yourself. Who knows why some people experience radical consciousness expansion while others don't. If you feel you have, great! What a gift. Enjoy it. Try not to take too much credit for it, though. Twist a few knobs on the machine that is your life, and it could have gone another way entirely.

The black belt of grace also invites us to trust deeper in God. When I find myself getting worked up at friends and family members still entrenched in theology that I find small and toxic, I try to step back and entrust their spiritual journey to God. My worrying and fretting about it won't do a thing. Just as I believe God guided me to where I am today, I choose to trust that other people's journeys are between them and God.

To the extent that you're able, try to relax. You've come so far. On your journey toward progressive Christianity, there will inevitably be a series of reckonings as you scrutinize the beliefs you once held dear. These reckonings can be painful, especially if you've wounded people you love as a direct result of beliefs you previously championed. How you respond to these reckonings, though, is entirely up to you. No, you cannot go back in time to undo that biting remark you made to your step-mom. You can't take back the years you made your gay neighbor feel like they were second class. And I can't track down the ninety-five people who attended Boycott Hell in 2001 and say, "Hey, remember that time I manipulated you into praying an oddly specific prayer? Yeah, sorry about that."

What you can do is show yourself kindness and grace, make peace with the normal and natural aspects of spiritual development, admit that you likely had no choice to be someone else anyway, anticipate that you'll continue to change because you haven't yet arrived, and extend all that kindness and grace to others, trusting that God knows and loves them even better than you do.

100

Shaking the Dust from Old Relationships

What to Do with Your Conservative (and "Concerned") Family and Friends

Without question, the number-one source of pain for those who've shifted toward a more progressive Christianity comes from the tension with friends and family who haven't made the same journey, and who think we've risked our salvation as a result. Show me one freshly shifted progressive Christian and I'll show you ten emails, texts, and Facebook comments from loved ones expressing their "concern." And that's just from Thursday.

We know well the disappointing look when we FaceTime with Dad while sitting next to our partner, or the anxious tone in Mom's voice when she calls to check in and casually drops a "So, have you been going to church lately?" We read between the lines when Pastor David, our youth leader from high school, vaguebooks about "praying for my former sheep who have wandered from the fold." We eventually stop opening emails from Grandpa Lawrence because we can't handle one more Max Lucado book recommendation or David Jeremiah sermon link, risking forever tainting our precious memories of playing at Papa's house when we were five.

Leading up to the writing of this book, as I told people "It's kind of like a survival guide for becoming a progressive Christian," almost without fail the responses included hope—if not desperation—that I would include a chapter like this one. For many of us, the pain of feeling like we've let the entire family down simply because we've wandered to a new part of the house in search of light to keep us warm pokes at us daily. And we don't know what to do about it. We don't know whether to sever communication entirely or to keep the lines open. We don't know whether to share with our family what we believe, or to smile and change the subject. We don't know whether we should block old friends on Facebook or stay in contact because, "I dunno, maybe I can help them see things differently?"

To make matters worse, thanks to the religious framework that fashioned you growing up, your mind gives conflicting messages on how to interpret these pains. Whereas a logical explanation might identify the pain as "This hurts because I love my family and I feel disconnected from them," we get stuck wondering "But what if it's the Holy Spirit convicting me because I walked away from the faith?" Yeah. That one hits home.

It's so damn confusing, and you're not alone in your tangled mess of emotions. Almost no one I've interacted with over the years feels like they've nailed this part of the Shift. Not everyone struggles to come to peace with who they used to be and how they used to believe. Not everyone experiences a war waged within them while their spiritual insides expand. But we almost all get flustered when attempting to maintain healthy relationships with the conservative community we no longer belong to.

Each person's context differs, but across the board, people I've met report feeling sad, confused, and lonely when shifting away from their conservative religious communities. There's no way to cover all the various scenarios, but I hope the following might be helpful for many. Also, I'm not a therapist. This book is no substitute for the insight and assistance you would gain from talking to a professional about your particular family dynamics. If nothing else, perhaps the ideas in this chapter become the catalyst you need to consider establishing new boundaries and practicing healthy self-care— both of which you might best accomplish under the direction of a therapist and/or spiritual director.

That being said, in my experience, the best thing you can do when navigating relationships with your more conservative friends and family is show up fully as yourself. Be open, vulnerable, and empowered with a range of grace-filled options depending on the kind of reaction you receive—whether positive or negative. To show what I mean, let's explore the story of Jesus sending out his friends "like sheep among wolves" (Matt 10:16).

THE FIRST SHORT-TERM MISSION TRIP

Four things stand out to me in Matthew 10 when Jesus sends his twelve disciples out on their first mission without him:

> These twelve Jesus sent out with the following instructions: "Do not go among the gentiles or enter any town of the Samaritans. Go rather to the lost sheep of Israel. As you go, proclaim this message: 'The kingdom of heaven has come near.' Heal the sick, raise the dead, cleanse those who have leprosy, drive out demons. Freely you have received; freely give. Do not get any gold or silver or copper to take with you in your

belts—no bag for the journey or extra shirt or sandals or a staff, for the worker is worth his keep. Whatever town or village you enter, search there for some worthy person and stay at their house until you leave. (Matthew 10: 5–11 NIV)

First, Jesus began by establishing where they should travel and on whom they should focus. The directions were clear: travel to Jewish towns, not to gentiles or Samaritans. This meant that the men and women the disciples would be engaging with were, in a very real sense, people from within their own communities. These were relatives and friends of friends, those with whom they shared values, customs, and religious ideas. Jesus sent his disciples on a mission, and their target audience was essentially their own demographic.

Second, the disciples were given two tasks: proclaim the nearness of the kingdom of heaven, and perform acts of liberation. Based on what we know of first-century religious practice and messianic expectations, it's safe to say that in the eyes of their audience, the disciples' mission would have been seen as progressive. That makes this a reasonable parallel to your own experience of returning home for the holidays and trying to explain to cousin Carl why you don't go to that one church any longer.

Third, Jesus wanted the disciples to fully rely on the hospitality of those they ministered to. This meant the twelve should show up in town completely empty-handed and open-hearted. They were to throw themselves at the mercy of others, trusting that people would care for them. What a vulnerable position! This was no arbitrary request, for I'm not sure you can adequately or accurately proclaim the nearness of God without *also* being fully vulnerable and open in the process.

Finally, I am moved by how deeply the disciples must have been convinced in the life-giving way of Jesus, apparently ready and willing to give their actual lives for it. After imparting his instructions, Jesus warned the disciples about the dangers awaiting them. Verses 16–42 recite reason after reason why this short-term mission trip was the worst idea ever. He confessed to sending them out like sheep among wolves, predicting they would encounter no shortage of persecution—including arrest, flogging, being disowned by family (sound familiar?), and possibly even death.

WHEN NO ONE WANTS YOUR SHOEHORN

Instructed to show up vulnerable, open, and reliant solely on strangers' hospitality, the disciples had their marching orders. But then Jesus told his friends to pay close attention to how people responded. Nestled between the mission directives and the predictions of impending suffering, Jesus equipped his followers with two proper reactions according to how their hosts might receive them. A response for their response, if you will.

"As you enter the home," Jesus said, "give it your greeting" (v. 12). In other words, they were to assume the role of initiators. They were to meet people where they were with openness, kindness, and respect. "If the home is deserving, let your peace rest on it; if it is not, let your peace return to you" (v. 13). The disciples were under no obligation to force their peace, message, ideas, and acts of liberation onto those they would encounter. If a home or community was open to them and provided hospitality and safety, they were to respond with gratitude and grace. Should the disciples encounter hostility, or should the home or village refuse them hospitality, thereby rejecting their dignity and devaluing their worth, Jesus instructed the disciples to let their peace return to them.

It's kind of like when you bring a gift you believe is awesome to a white elephant party but all night long you watch as people pass it over. "Fine," you say, "if no one wants this hand-crafted ebony shoehorn engraved with Daffy Duck, I'll take it."

Then Jesus goes one step further. Not only do you take your Daffy Duck shoehorn back, but you leave the party altogether and refuse to accept the party favor the host wants to force on you. "If anyone will not welcome you or listen to your words, leave that home or town and *shake the dust off your feet*" (v. 14, emphasis mine).

It is here, in the center of the Venn diagram of Florence + the Machine, Taylor Swift, and Jesus of Nazareth, that we discover a path for navigating the challenge of difficult relationships with our more conservative friends and family: Shake. It. Off.

ACCEPT THEIR REJECTION

You know that scene from *Monsters, Inc.* where a monster returned to the scare floor after a disastrous attempt at scaring a child only to discover the child's small white sock clung to his back? Immediately, a red alert blared, initiating code 2319. In swooped the Child Detection Agency (CDA) to secure the premises and decontaminate George Sanderson, the orange, single-horned scarer who brought human clothing into the monsters' world. The CDA tackled George to the ground, carefully extracted the sock with large metal tongs, and sealed it in a contraption designed to incinerate the dangerous article of clothing back into star dust. Though they decimated the sock, the CDA still needed to shave George of all his monster hair in the event any of the child's cooties remained. Returning to the realm of the monsters with any trace of the human world would endanger everyone.

That's what comes to mind when I hear Jesus tell his friends to "shake the dust from their feet" should they encounter people hostile to their presence. Scholars disagree on the precise meaning of this old Jewish idiom, but the general idea was, "I'm leaving this behind, because to take it with me would be hazardous." Like a sock stuck to George's back.

Bold, brazen, and a bit unexpected, Jesus gave his friends this response to empower them to face hostility with both grace and truth. It let them accept the rejection of those who would not receive them. This wasn't permission for the disciples to isolate themselves into like-minded bands of followers. Nor were they instructed to reject people in town right out of the gate if they held different ideas about dietary laws, temple taxes, and so on. The whole point is that they were to initiate contact, be the ones to show up open and vulnerable—then, if they experienced rejection, they were to respond by shaking the dust off their feet. If their openness and vulnerability were not met in loving and welcome embrace, then Jesus's suggestion (perhaps even *command?*) was to say yes to their no. Shake it off, and move on.

When such scenarios took place, it was the *disciples* being rejected, not the other way around. This distinction is key.

It's not uncommon when journeying through the Shift to hear from those within our old communities that our movement toward progressive Christianity is a rejection of them—the people and the relationships. Deep in our hearts, however, we know that our rejection is rooted not in the people (whom we love) but in the beliefs and attitudes and behaviors that we can no longer get behind. Conversely, our experience is that it is *we* who are met with inhospitable postures, no longer welcome at the table. And in those moments of personal rejection, I wonder if Jesus's invitation to say yes to their no is exactly what our well-being needs.

The charge to shake the dust off their feet provided Jesus's disciples a healthier and more peaceful alternative to fighting back (e.g., "You *will* hear our message and accept our healing, dangit!") or remaining in place as doormats, passive recipients of perpetual rejection. Jesus knew what all enlightened people know: you cannot control how other people act. Which is why he gave his disciples the next best thing, a demonstrable action they were fully capable of carrying out so they could stop casting their pearls before swine and move on to a place that would receive them.

THIS IS YOUR BED, YOU LIE IN IT

It might sound harsh at first, but I believe this principle of shaking off the dust offers us a powerful path forward when we encounter the obstacle of constant tension and conflict with our more conservative friends and family members.

In life, all we can hope to control are our own thoughts and actions, and that's hard enough. It's an illusion—a dangerous one at that—to think we might be able to control or change how our friends and family think. The power in the act of shaking the dust from our feet is how it communicates both what I'm doing for myself and what I'm no longer doing for you. For my own well-being, I am leaving. I will not stay here as a willing participant in your nonacceptance. And this dust, a residue of your rejection, I'm leaving it here too. I refuse to take it with me and thereby remain enslaved by your disapproval.

To shake the dust from your feet says, "This connection between us is unhealthy. I have vulnerably opened up to you, but instead of welcoming me or showing me respect as a fellow beloved child of God, you made it clear I am unwelcome. You reject my ideas, my questions, and my concerns. More than that (as many LGBTQ people know so well), you have rejected me as a human. This has gone beyond simply disagreeing into a place of hostility. You have attacked me, blamed me, made accusations against me, and refused to give me space to be seen or heard. For me to remain in this relationship would not be healthy, so I'm out. As I shake the dust off my feet, I am declaring that your accusations and your attempts to shame me will no longer succeed. You have decided I'm not welcome.

You have caused this division between us, and I am not responsible for mending that. It's not my job to fix us, and it's certainly not my job to fix you. In spite of my posture of humility and earnest desire to connect with you, you have chosen to remain fixed in your old ways, refusing to consider that maybe you don't have everything figured out. In your fear of new information or new ideas, you closed the door on me. On us. That is the bed you have made, now I leave you to lie in it."

Whew . . . yeah, feel free to pause and take a breath.

By the way, sometimes rejection from our old friends and family looks more like ghosting than slamming a door in your face. Lots of progressive Christians report that when they left their faith communities, they weren't met with pitchforks and Bible-thumping so much as silence and avoidance. When I got fired in Arizona and exited the church abruptly, most people never bothered to say goodbye. There's a unique type of pain in being ignored by a community you spent over five years ministering to. One family, months after the fact, responded to one of my emails and explained, "Look, no offense, but the center of our friendship was our relationship through the church." At the time, that was hard to hear. But, looking back, I now respect their honesty and appreciate that I heard *anything* from them at all. Turns out, I prefer direct rejection over a spiritualized silent treatment.

FOUR CHALLENGES TO SHAKING THE DUST

None of this is easy, by the way. Lest my impassioned pleas to shake the dust deceive you, I know this stuff is undeniably hard. These are real relationships with real people—people you love and who have been a major part of your life. Shaking the dust might come across as cold and ungenerous, but I assure you that love can be both its driving factor and its main ingredient. There is a difference between the Christ pattern of dying to yourself so that you might be reborn, and being a victim of someone else's intolerance and fear. It's not always an easily discernible difference, I'll grant you that. But the better we can learn to identify which is which (or find a therapist who will see it more clearly than we can), the better off we'll be.

If you find it overwhelming to even imagine initiating the shaking of dust from relationships in your life, you're not alone and you're not a failure. This stuff is hard. To help normalize this, here are four factors that contribute to just how challenging this process can be.

1. CLUNKY. Shaking the dust off your feet is clunky because most people are not well-practiced in the art of setting (and keeping) boundaries, especially with family and other close relationships. Many who grew up in more conservative Christian homes (myself included) have a degree of arrested emotional development in part because natural and normal emotions (such as anger) were seen as unspiritual. As a result, we did a lot of suppressing and spiritual bypassing (using spiritual ideas to avoid or explain away unresolved emotional issues and psychological wounds, a way to check out instead of check in). Finding the words—let alone the fortitude—to express that we won't be subject to any more shaming or accusations is incredibly clunky. A good therapist or targeted reading on the topic can support you in clearly articulating what you need.

2. UNCLEAR. How can we tell the difference between genuine disagreement done in mutual respect versus, I don't know, how you often end up feeling after leaving your sister's house? They keep insisting they respect you, the choices you've made, and what you believe nowadays. And yet every time they mention some statistic about how kids need both a mom *and* a dad your gut tells you a different story. Part of what makes it so hard to know if or when to shake the dust off your feet is this sort of murkiness. There isn't always a clear distinction between what are normal challenges that arise within any type of close relationship, and what are patterns of mistreatment and dehumanization that render the relationship unsafe. In these cases, it's often helpful to tell a trusted friend about your experiences. If they start freaking out and wondering why you're letting yourself be treated that way, that could indicate that it's time to shake some dust.

3. COUNTERINTUITIVE. I say it's counterintuitive because there is a strong undercurrent in Christianity to be bridge builders. We have been preconditioned to think the most Christlike posture is one that continually shows up and tries to connect and make peace (as though peace in this context means complete reconciliation). Which is why shaking the dust from our feet can conjure objections such as, *Is this really what Jesus would do?* Yes, he would! That's the point of this chapter.

4. PAINFUL. Perhaps the biggest reason why so many people don't do more dust-shaking is because it's painful. Short and simple. Here I am, safely behind my keyboard, suggesting that you walk away from some of the most meaningful relationships in your life. *Yeah, sure, Colby. I'll get right on that.* I hear you and I feel you. Easier said than done. Who wants to make the choice between not having a parent in their life versus having a parent around who's constantly jabbing at you and picking fights? Where's the obvious choice in that? There isn't one, I'm afraid. Often, we endure the pain of unhealthy relationships because the pain of not having the relationship at all strikes us as unbearable. If it feels like managing relationships with our more conservative friends and family is a lose-lose scenario, that's because it often is. On one hand, we would suffer the loss of a meaningful relationship. On the other, we endure the loss of dignity, self-care, and our freedom to flourish gets stifled.

When we truly count the costs, however, maintaining relationships with people who hold you back from becoming the best possible you ultimately poses the greater threat to your well-being.

A REALISTIC ROUTE

I'm not advocating you leave at the first sign of discomfort or disagreement. I'm all for having grit and resilience. Yes, sometimes it's absolutely the right call to hang in there and declare that you're not going anywhere. This can be a powerful statement, like Kumail Nanjiani in *The Big Sick* showing up at his parents' house for dinner and stubbornly announcing, "I've decided I won't let you kick me out of the family." But in my experience, and in the stories I've heard from others, this tenacious posture of "Here I am, you can't get rid of me" is only effective if we pair it with both healthy boundaries (at least, on your side of the fence) and a grounded sense of your true identity. Once we find our footing, confident in the truth that we are a loved child of God—*full stop*—*then* we can show up in difficult spaces more likely to withstand whatever jabs or passive-aggressive questions come our way. It is only from this empowered and grounded place that we can vulnerably open ourselves to announce, "I am here, asking you to receive me. I will respect both myself and you by accepting whatever response you give, be it hospitable welcome or painful rejection."

I'm also not suggesting that shaking off the dust implies permanent separation. Establishing new and healthy boundaries might be necessary for a season, but you may need to reexamine them down the road to see if they still make sense. Shaking off the dust might be only the first step, albeit a necessary one to give you space to breathe, heal, and grow. But it doesn't mean you won't someday be open to knocking on their door again.

To that end, in the event you do choose to explore reengaging with a relationship that previously required dust-shaking, your upgraded worldview as a progressive Christian benefits you greatly. One of the things I've noticed as a result of the Shift is a newfound ability to more easily separate a person from their beliefs. This affords you increased capacity to interact with (and show love to) someone with whom you disagree on a number of issues.

For example, you could imagine how this new superpower makes showing up to family reunions easier for you than, say, for your more conservative relatives. Because you are now able to separate Uncle Jake's belief about a literal six-day creation from the fact that he is as much a loved child of God as you are. But when a person is convinced that their standing with God hinges on correct belief (like Uncle Jake and the rest of the family in this scenario), then ideas or questions that challenge those beliefs feel scary and threatening. Not only do your new ideas about evolution make Uncle Jake feel uneasy, but in his mind your heretical beliefs place *you* outside the family of God. So, now he's scared *of* you and scared *for* you. Such a climate of fear and anxiety does not sound like my idea of a good time. But if you've gone through a season (perhaps precipitated by shaking the dust off your feet) of grounding yourself in the truth that you are loved, that you are okay, and that you are free, then at least now you might be able to imagine walking into the lion's den with your head held high, ready to hand out grace and love to all.

Now, there's a massive exception to that last paragraph. If you exited or were kicked out of your conservative community because you are LGBTQ and your sexual orientation or gender expression were unwelcome, or because you're a woman who could no longer exist in an ecosystem relegating you to an inferior status, then showing back up to family reunions or accepting your old small group's dinner party invitation becomes infinitely more complicated—and for good reason. I'm reminded of the words of activist and writer Robert Jones Jr.: "We can disagree and still love each other unless your disagreement is rooted in my oppression and denial of my humanity and right to exist."[1] Sure, you can separate your grandma's identity as a loved daughter of God from her belief that only Christians will get raptured and go to heaven. But it's a whole other ball game to set aside your brother's insistence that because you're gay you cannot be a Christian, or because you lack certain genitalia you should not be leading or teaching men. In such cases, not only does shaking the dust off your feet become necessary for survival, but you might need to keep your hard boundaries in place until your friends or family have softened their hearts or changed their minds. Do not continue to give people the gift of your presence if they cannot give you the gift of your humanity.

Dear readers, if you've ever shown up on someone's doorstep and made yourself vulnerable, seeking their hospitality, acceptance, and peace, but instead received rejection or shaming, I am so sorry. That was wrong and you did not deserve it. I empathize with the instinct you might have to try to build bridges or reconcile. It's natural to take familiar Christian principles such as sacrificial love and forgiveness, reflect on how to live them out, and then get all twisted up and conclude that the way of Christ would never look like ending a relationship. But I think that's a fundamental misunderstanding of what the life and teachings of Jesus reveal to us about relationships.

I offer you this permission slip, should you need it. You hereby have permission to create new and healthier boundaries with the people in your life who will not accept you as you are nor hold space for your beliefs. It is okay to shake the dust from your feet when they reject you.

---

1 Robert Jones Jr. (@SonofBaldwin), Twitter, August 18, 2015, 10:19 a.m., https://tinyurl.com/y55ubs9y.

It is hard, but it is good.

In fact, it might be the only realistic route toward the possibility of one day having an authentic relationship with them built on genuine acceptance, mutual respect, and true vulnerability.

A NOTE TO THE CONSERVATIVE READER

If you are reading this book from the perspective of a more conservative Christian, hoping to understand the heart and mind of a loved one who has gone down the path toward progressive Christianity, first let me say: thank you. Your efforts to understand your loved one create the building blocks for showing true love.

Maybe you're reading this in desperation, a final attempt to understand your son or daughter. Maybe you're reading this in curiosity because you genuinely can't wrap your head around why your friend has "left the faith." Whatever the reason, you're doing it, and that's amazing. Thank you.

I also want you to know (if you haven't picked up from this chapter already) just how much you are loved by the person who bought this book and feverishly turned to this chapter, anxious for help with how to navigate their relationship with you. I'm sure there are moments when you question their love for you because, after all, if they really loved you, why would they [insert any number of beliefs or actions you find troubling or dangerous here]. Please know that their decision to follow the voice inside them—what I would call the prompting of the spirit, what Abraham heard when he left his father and mother's home to traverse the unknown—isn't about you. They are not choosing this path to spite you, though perhaps it feels that way. No, they love you, and they long for the day when you can share a cup of tea and talk openly and honestly about your differences, each holding space for the other to be seen and heard.

When Progressives Attack

What to Do When Fellow Progressives Get Critical

Those on the journey toward becoming a progressive Christian suffer quite the shock when experiencing friendly fire for the first time. Even though the core values of the progressive worldview include tolerance, love, acceptance, and critical thinking, progressive Christians are not exempt from judgmental attitudes and exclusionary actions. Ridicule from other progressives feels jarring, and I wouldn't fault you for assuming that leaving behind your conservative communities also might've meant leaving behind judgment, narrow-mindedness, and an inability to hold space for differing opinions. Turns out, such shortcomings are unavoidable features of what it means to be human, regardless of what side of the spectrum you call home.

If you haven't already been on the receiving end of such criticism, prepare yourself. For very good reasons—as I'll explore in the coming pages—landmines abound as you traverse the new terrain of progressive circles. You might be happily going along, say, contributing to an online discussion or sharing a thought in your small group, when out of nowhere you trip a landmine and suffer the shrapnel of someone suddenly insisting you're part of the problem. You stare in disbelief, unsure how to proceed, and can't for the life of you figure out why people you assumed were on the same team are now firing shots your way.

Before getting to a few of the survival tips when it comes to navigating the friendly fire of fellow progressive Christians, we need to clear out the weeds that often ensnare us in such interactions. Progressive Christian fratricide can occur when our own values distort and work against us. When we hyper-focus on core ideas—even if they're good ideas—we run the risk of veering toward a type of progressive fundamentalism driven by a vision of ideological purity.

IN SEARCH OF BALANCE, MODERATION, AND NUANCE

Many of us who came out of conservative Christianity (especially the evangelical variety) recall purity culture, the shame-filled collection of beliefs surrounding sex and sexuality. A similar culture of purity exists in progressive circles, but instead of revolving around masturbation and premarital sex, it uses metrics such as political correctness, owning and checking your privilege, and varying levels of awareness. Some of the more frustrating interactions progressive Christians have with one another occur as a result of violating this (often unspoken) creed of ideological purity. When this happens, we find ourselves playing with the fire of fundamentalism, albeit of the progressive flavor.

You'd think we left such infighting behind, but such is the danger of any group that hyper-focuses on its own views and remains unaware of the very real possibility of descending toward extremism. And extremism can feel great, right up until it doesn't. If left unchecked, extreme views in any direction can cause harm as the implications and demands of what it means to actually live out such extremism inevitably leads to either self-ruin, violence to others, or both.

Fundamentalism is a type of extremism, and progressives can be fundamentalists just as much as conservatives. In a fundamentalist worldview, purity to the group's ideals serves as the ultimate criterion by which you're deemed in or out, with us or against us. Diluting the group's creeds with words or actions deemed inappropriate by either the gatekeepers or the mob will put you on the fast track for banishment. In spite of our value of openness, extreme progressives can demand a singular adherence to particular beliefs, and in the process squash out space for people to feel differently. Questioning the methods by which some members of the in-group practice their values is darn near anathema. I've seen progressive Christians fall prey to the same insistence many of us escaped, namely that our group holds claim to the one true interpretation. Fundamentalism rejects outside opinions and inquiry, and chastises anyone on the inside for failing to fall in line. This leads its devotees to either a lemming-like plunge off the cliff or a snakelike consumption of their own tails.

In order to avoid such outcomes, we need balance, moderation, questioning, nuance, and tolerance—all qualities despised by extremism—because too much of anything, even if it's good, will inevitably result in diminishing returns. My nine-year-old son intuited this the other day when, upon returning home from family vacation, his younger brother exclaimed, "I wish we could be on vacation every day!" My nine-year-old replied, "But if every day was awesome, then no days would be awesome."

Progressive Christianity, my home base for the past decade, requires heavy doses of balancing out if it wants to survive as a movement. The yin-yang of Taoism has it right. Yin—the black side with the white dot—represents darkness, cold, negativity, chaos, and passivity. Yang—the white side with the black dot—represents lightness, warmth, positivity, order, and action. The two sides complement and balance each other. Simple, yet profound. Where one pushes, the other makes space. Where one retracts, the other fills.[1] Not only that, but the contrasting dots on either side remind us that you cannot have one without the other; if there's only one side, then everything collapses. You're utterly lost in both extremes, whether total darkness *or* total light. You'll be annihilated in either condition, pure heat *or* pure cold.

When I've been attacked by other progressives (or when I'm the attacker, which I'm certainly guilty of), it's usually a symptom of leaving no space for nuance or tension. We only push, and we don't leave space to be pulled. We bail on the both/and, then descend into either/or. Such a posture cannot lead us where we want to go—if where we want to go involves creating an inclusive and charitable community defined by love and advocating for justice.

Look, we've all been swept up in a mob of call-out culture. It feels good to tweet that savage takedown of some so-called progressive politician, author, or leader. We used to grab pitchforks for those who got divorced, had an abortion, or married someone of the same gender. Now we sharpen our spears when someone

---

1 "Correlatives in Chinese philosophy are not opposites, mutually excluding each other. They represent the ebb and flow of the forces of reality: yin/yang, male/female; excess/ defect; leading/following; active/passive. As one approaches the fullness of yin, yang begins to horizon and emerge and vice versa." Ronnie Littlejohn, "Daoist Philosophy," Internet Encyclopedia of Philosophy, www.iep.utm.edu/daoism.

unearths an inappropriate tweet that a prominent person posted ten years ago (that they clearly wouldn't subscribe to today, so where's the space to let people grow and change?), or when someone dares admit to appreciate the work of people who don't pass the progressive values purity test (I'm looking at you, Jordan Peterson, Taylor Swift, and Chris Pratt), or when we think a particular board or panel or group doesn't have the correct diversity of representation (even though there's limited slots, so which group gets left out?).

Lest you think I'm being too flippant, I am wholeheartedly behind efforts to diversify leadership, to call people to task for their harmful words, and to choose to walk away from people or companies over a significant clash in values. But a lot of gray space exists between total acceptance and utter rejection, between complete failure and sheer perfection. Not to mention that we all have our own unique criteria or issues that trigger our outrage. Internal conflict within communities such as progressive Christians often emerges when we assume everyone else must have our same standards, metrics of justice, and ideas of what is good and what is bad. Not only is that absurd, but it's unrealistic. Yet, we continue to snipe at one another and divide over relatively minor differences, forgetting the much larger areas of shared values that should bind us together.

When we lock down an extreme position on anything and refuse to hold space for nuance, we paint ourselves into a corner where the only road out leads through hypocrisy. In response to sexual assault allegations surrounding figures such as Alabama Governor Roy Moore, Supreme Court Justice Brett Kavanaugh, and of course Donald Trump, many Democrat leaders publicly adopted a zero-tolerance posture. The near-unanimous call for Minnesota Senator Al Franken to resign amid allegations of sexual misconduct showed the fruit of such a posture. But a year later, when three of Virginia's top state officials (who's positions were far more politically critical and needed than Senator Franken's) were caught in serious allegations regarding both sexual misconduct and racism, many of the same zero-tolerance Democrats suddenly went silent. Demonstrating that extreme, zero-tolerance positions might be, in the real world, untenable (or, as in this instance, subject to the whims of convenience).

When we reject the many shades of gray that make up the world we live in, and when we neglect to season our positions with a dash of nuance (and then view others as weaker or less committed to a cause if they insist on a more nuanced position), we ensure that one day the tables will turn on us. And when they do, the only options will be either hypocrisy or doubling down and further isolating ourselves.

GETTING WOKE ON WOKE

In the mid-2010s, the term *woke* emerged among progressives as a helpful shorthand to describe the important empathetic work in understanding the realities of the oppressed. To be woke implied you had more awareness than you used to (because it's a process, not a destination) regarding systemic injustices perpetuated against communities such as black people, LGBTQ individuals, and women. Staying woke meant committing to keeping your eyes open, vigilant to how those in power bend the playing field to keep the marginalized in the margins.

Quickly, however, many progressives (myself included) needed to become woke about the term itself so as to avoid the pitfall of cultural appropriation. The term originated and took shape within black vernacular (such as Erykah Badu's hook "I stay woke" in her 2008 song "Master Teacher"), and then crept into mainstream use, primarily as a hashtag in social media posts responding to racial justice issues, most notably the #BlackLivesMatter movement.

I bring this up for two reasons. First, it illuminates an important aspect of the journey toward becoming a progressive *person* (let alone a progressive Christian). Jesus focused his kingdom work on those whom society pushed to the edges. Liberation theologians such as Gustavo Gutiérrez taught us how the gospels reveal God's preferential option for the poor, those on the underside of power. When Christians wake up to this aspect of Jesus's life and work (what conservative Christians sometimes pejoratively call "the social gospel"), the result can be shocking. Many of us slept on systemic injustice, both unaware of and benefitting from the ways in which our society privileges particular ethnicities, genders, orientations, and socioeconomic classes. When our faith—both in the creedal sense and as a practice—expands to include more people who don't look, think, or act like us, the frigid-cold reality snaps us out of our cozy, limited versions of Christianity and American life. For many of us, the journey toward progressive Christianity went hand in hand with waking up to what has been going on for a very long time.

The other reason I bring up the idea of woke is because it illustrates how clunky discourse within progressive circles can be. In this instance, well-intentioned progressive people came across the term and felt it perfectly articulated their experience of finally seeing the realities of systemic injustice. It was then used in conversation (both online and in real life) as a descriptive contrast to their previous head-in-the-sand state. Unfortunately, through a lack of understanding and a lack of practice in researching a concept before adopting it, we held little regard for how appropriating such a term can run the risk of centering whiteness—a key pillar that needs to be dismantled in our efforts to eradicate white supremacy.

The argument is sound: white people using the term *woke* can be inappropriate. It's an example of how blackness gets used, misused, and appropriated by white folk. I completely agree. At the same time, I also agree with the argument that language is constantly evolving, and the term *woke* has grown to include other forms of inequality and oppression, thereby opening it up to a wider audience for increased contexts. And I think that's a good thing. It's both/and. But I've seen time and time again how progressives struggle to hold the both/and. (Even now, I feel some of you pulling back, unhappy with me, preferring I come down and stay on the side of "White people shouldn't say *woke*," and say nothing of merit regarding the other perspectives.)

This pattern happens often within progressivism. We spiral out and get stuck in conversations in which we criticize and attack people for taking a slightly different approach or holding a slightly different conviction. Rather than stepping back and remembering that we are ultimately on the same team, all fighting to smash the patriarchy, dismantle white supremacy, end LGBTQ injustice, and so on. We snipe at one another over who isn't checking their privilege enough, who is too sensitive, who isn't doing it right, and so on.

The point is not that we shouldn't challenge one another or shouldn't attempt to help our friends and family better understand a given issue. The point is that these conversations are inherently difficult because they deal with real lives and real people who have been legitimately harmed. We won't always get it right, for instance, when talking about transgender people, racial injustice, or immigration issues. But in our call-out culture, where we are quick to cancel a person the first time they step out of line and defile the purity of progressive ideology, we sacrifice the possibility of truly building a vast coalition of progressively minded people—all for the quick high of taking someone down and getting patted on the back for it.

When we flatten perspectives into an either/or dichotomy, we betray the fact that such toxic dualism was part of why we left conservative Christianity in the first place.

WHAT TO DO WHEN PROGRESSIVES ATTACK

Progressives wage attacks on other progressives they deem either not progressive enough or not progressive in the right way. Discerning when to dodge those attacks (and not get caught up in the fight) and when to humbly accept their strikes (and thereby learn from the pain) can not only determine your own survival, but it can improve the overall health and well-being of your new communities. When progressives attack—and they will—I suggest we conduct ourselves with:

+ Open eyes (be aware of other's pain)
+ Soft hearts (be a safe place for the wounded)
+ Understanding ears (listen compassionately)
+ Synergized speech (respect both intent and impact)
+ Resolute spine (refuse to quit when it gets hard)

1. OPEN EYES. Battered and bruised, the demographics of many progressive landscapes consist of groups of people familiar with discrimination and oppression. Long accustomed to being used, ignored, or marginalized, many carry wounds either on or just below the surface. Like your friend who winces when you hug them because they have a deep sunburn under their clothes that you cannot see, it's not uncommon to accidentally step in it when navigating progressive circles. This is why many people on the right use the term "snowflakes" to name how easy it is to ruffle the feathers of liberals. In using such a term, they fundamentally misunderstand what makes many progressives sensitive. What they see as fragile and easily offended, I see as sympathetic to the pain of others and a deep longing for justice. Progressives aren't fragile—in fact, they're some of the strongest, most resilient people you'll ever meet. It's not about walking on eggshells, but knowing the very real pain from people's stories can equip us to enter conversations more hospitably.

One Sunday I gave a sermon extolling the virtues of agape love, pointing out the revolutionary quality of laying down your needs for another. At one point I observed how this kind of love is counter-instinctual and goes against our natural inclination for self-preservation. Afterwards, I heard from several women in the church (including my wife) who shared their discomfort with parts of my sermon. They explained how most women—especially those who grew up in religious homes—were groomed by their communities to always self-sacrifice. The revolutionary posture for many women looks more like *establishing* their needs, not laying them down. My failure to name that, or to at least hold space for how my words might land differently for many of the women in the audience, not only worked against the point I was trying to make, but it also reinforced some painful messages in the minds of people I love.

Part of the work in becoming a progressive Christian involves entering conversations with eyes wide open to the history, pain, and ways in which different people have experienced life. As a friend of mine once said, if we know folks are walking around still carrying buckets of gasoline forced upon them by the oppressive systems and choices of others, then the least we could do is not throw matches in their general direction.

2. SOFT HEARTS. If you leave a marshmallow on the counter, eventually the starch molecules, meticulously aligned during the cooking process, slowly come undone. This results in the squishy white square going stale and hard. However, you can seal that hard marshmallow inside a ziplock bag alongside a piece of bread, and within a day or two the marshmallow will regain its softness.

Some progressive Christians are like that hardened marshmallow, and for good reasons. Burned by religion, betrayed by people we loved, and disillusioned with ideas of who we thought God is and what life should be like, many people erect protective walls and create a hardened exterior designed for defense. Even if their wounds weren't caused directly by the church, our culture perpetuates enough suffering for minorities, women, LGBTQ people, and other marginalized groups to justify such hardened, skeptical armor.

One of the biggest ways we can show up for one another is simply by remaining in one another's presence and refusing to be pushed or scared away. Like the bread in the ziplock bag, your proximity to their pain, free of judgment or abandonment, carries enormous potential to realign the patterns in their brain that default to a protective posture. Bearing witness to one another's experience and holding their pain with them can dissolve their defenses and help restore them to a tender, soft state.

The next time you find yourself on the receiving end of friendly fire, consider that maybe this is a moment to be the bread for someone else's marshmallow.

3. UNDERSTANDING EARS. In addition to showing up and sitting in someone else's pain with them, one of the greatest gifts (and possibly the most important work many of us can do) is a commitment to listening well and, like the prayer of Saint Francis, seeking first to understand rather than to be understood.

Thich Nhat Hanh, in his book *Going Home: Jesus and Buddha as Brothers*, suggests that understanding is the ground of love. We access the ability to love others—including our enemies, as Jesus would have it—when we start with a desire to understand them. *Who are they? Where are they coming from? What has shaped their life? Why might they see the world as they do?* Understanding leads to compassion as we begin to see how *of course* they respond in that way, or act like this, or feel as they do. People are the way they are for a damn good reason, and listening to them and their stories can open space for us to understand what those reasons are.

Compassion emerges not only when we begin to understand why people are the way they are, but even more so when we accept that, given all the same circumstances, *we* would likely be no different. When we get frustrated with other people, we tend to think we'd do this differently or act like that instead. Such thinking totally bypasses the very real probability that if you were born and raised exactly as they were (same parents/religion/ethnicity/culture/economics/etc.), then you would almost certainly think and act and talk like them. We tend to hold others to a standard of our own creation, informed by our own background, indifferent to the diverse struggles we all face.

Listening helps us understand, understanding leads to compassion, and compassion opens the way for love. Suddenly, we see others not as our enemies, not as people out to get us, but as people for whom we do not desire suffering. We now feel a longing for their well-being in the same way we hope for our own. We may still not like what they're saying, and it may still be appropriate to push back, but now you're engaging in the conversation from a place of love, and that changes everything.

4. SYNERGIZED SPEECH. Some interactions can go south by failing to hold two concepts in mind: impact and intent. When you are talking with someone, whether online or in real life, how your words land with them matters. We carry responsibility for how our words—as well as our posture and tone—impact the people we interact with. At the same time, our intentions, the spirit from which we are coming from, also matters. Healthy communication emerges from synergizing these two components and respecting the role they each play.

When progressive people overplay the importance of impact (which happens a lot) and insist that intent is irrelevant, we are only inhaling and not exhaling. Knowing a person's intent gives you valuable insight into where their heart is, in addition to a sense of what to expect from them moving forward. If I'm walking down the street and you crash into me, the impact of that collision might result in me falling to the ground in pain with a busted ankle and bleeding hands. In one sense, whether you meant to makes no difference regarding my wounds. On the other hand, if you intended to do me harm, well, now I know you're not a safe person and I'll avoid you in the future. But if it were a complete accident because, say, you were phalking (walking while looking at your phone), now you're in a different bucket in my mental storage space. Because I loathe phalking (seriously, people, just stop walking for a second and step to the side!), I might be annoyed at you, but clearly your intent was not to cause me great harm. You're clumsy, not cruel. I've seen many progressive people in progressive spaces insisting that intent doesn't matter, but their arguments never hold up.

At the same time, a person might double down on their intent, insisting that you shouldn't be upset "if you only knew where I'm coming from." This blatant refusal to take any ownership for the impact of their words reeks of entitled ignorance. You don't get to ramble through a china store swinging lightsabers with your child, then call the store clerk crazy for getting upset that you broke seventeen plates. Your amazing intentions to spend quality time with your offspring, while admirable, doesn't free you from taking responsibility for the damage you caused. Empathy demands we try to feel what the other person is feeling, even if they're in pain as a result of your good intention.

Both impact and intent matter. Both contribute to whether any given interaction becomes productive or destructive. You might say or do something that genuinely triggers another person's pain, and the least helpful response is to defend your intent while ignoring the impact. Likewise, begin with a gracious posture toward those who wound you, because their intent may have been to do anything but.

5. RESOLUTE SPINE. I've had my fair share of being on the receiving end of progressive ire. When I wrote my book criticizing the Christian tradition for misusing the Bible to justify discrimination against LGBTQ people, I was accused by many progressives of building a platform off the struggle of gay people and centering my straightness. I've sat in gatherings and conferences listening to POC speakers openly criticize white leaders (like myself) for the ways in which planting churches, speaking at conferences, and accepting book contracts continues to center whiteness and support white supremacy. And, as mentioned earlier, more than once women have told me how what I said perpetuates misogynistic narratives.

Every one of these opinions and critiques have merit. My initial reaction to almost all these experiences began with defensiveness and an insistence of my good intentions. I am growing by learning to take people's criticism, hear their frustrations, and hold space for their reasonable and well-earned grievances. I'm learning to better sit with their words and learn from them. As Maya Angelou famously said, "I did then what I knew how to do. Now that I know better, I do better." The invitation for me is not to fall prey to some victim mentality ("Poor me!") or throw in the towel because it's too hard ("Well, fine, I'm out").

One Sunday at our church during Black History Month, the band led a rousing rendition of one of the Civil Rights Movement's anthems, "Ain't Gonna Let Nobody Turn Me Around." The song, a rally cry for refusing to let any person, discrimination, or oppression turn us around from our focused march toward freedom, convicted me to my core. I had to stop singing at one point to face the reckoning that I, a straight, white male, generally *do* get turned around when I face opposition or what feels to me like unfair treatment. For progressive Christians who, like me, possess layers of privilege, we can learn a lot from the Selmas, the Stonewalls, and the Seneca Falls: moments in history when marginalized people stood up to power, refusing to be turned around. I'm so accustomed to the world being slanted in my favor that sometimes, if I endure the slightest bit of struggle or a hint of pushback, I crumble like Liston in the first.

But I'm learning the importance of having a strong back to go with my soft front.[2] The work of many of us who identify as progressive Christians—tearing down unjust systems, building compassionate communities, raising brave and kind children, advocating for the underserved, healing the hurting—is far too important for me tap out when the going gets hard.

My great hope for progressive Christianity rests upon the power of honest, humble, and charitable conversations. We must do our absolute best to believe in one another's good intentions, and trust that we want the same things. We will disagree on how we achieve our goals, and that's okay. Diversity in practice is just as important as diversity in belief. We must show one another that we are willing to listen, learn, and show compassion. We must model for the rest of the world what gracious dialogue looks like. We must ask good questions, ask the right people, and assume they have something to teach us. We must forgive quickly when offense is taken, and not waste one more minute on hurt feelings. Too much is at stake.

---

2 Thanks to Brené Brown in *Braving the Wilderness* for this powerful imagery.

Families fight. It's okay. But may we choose mercy over sacrifice, and inclusion over exclusion, so that together we might all work for the greater good.

12

Stay Open, My Friends

Why I Remain a Christian

My friend's face beamed more than usual as he rushed over to share the news. Our church service had just ended, and while people milled about, catching up or stacking away the chairs, my friend gushed joy as he shouted over the house music. I knew how his parents had firmly disapproved of his coming out as gay years ago, making it clear that any future boyfriend would not be welcome at their home. But that morning, my friend wept as he shared how his mom recently did an about-face. Not only did she express excitement to meet his boyfriend, but she spoke of her desire to love and welcome him in the same way she did her daughter-in-law. "She's not fully affirming yet," he said, still smiling, "but her feelings have totally shifted."

As this survival guide comes to a close, I share that story for two reasons. First, I'm sure you have people in your life who cannot understand the Shift you've made, and who perhaps remain a source of distress for you. You feel like the theological chasm separating you will never close, forever impacting your capacity for meaningful connection. Full disclosure: that might be true. You might spend the rest of your days struggling to navigate those rocky waters.

But remember that you, before you shifted and began a journey toward progressive Christianity, likely never would have foreseen your own change either. From your current vantage point, you might reflect back and feel like you simply followed where logic, reason, or common sense led you. This is faulty thinking (I'll explain more below). At some point, you were carried away by a vision of a more expansive, generous, and compassionate approach to the world. You never know when that same wind might animate someone else. You never know what's going on in the hearts and minds of those you might assume will never change. People *do* change. *You've* changed. So, I challenge you to hold loosely your expectations for the future mindsets of those close to you. I think the wisest move involves choosing to trust that the God who whisked you and me along in our lives to where we are now is the same animating force present in the lives of our loved ones.

The other reason I tell this story now is because it reminds me that the head cannot go where the heart is unwilling. An emotional opening necessarily precedes an intellectual commitment to a novel idea. We think reason and logic lead us to our convictions, but the truth is we feel a particular way first, then we find evidence to support it. Even though my friend, shouting over the house music that Sunday morning, was quick to point out that his mom was not yet theologically affirming of his sexuality, I affirmed the significance of her change of heart. She now at least possesses the potential to reassess her long-held views on faith and sexuality—something she could not have done beforehand.

An open heart opens the door for an open mind.

REMAIN OPEN

In picking up this book and seeking guidance for becoming a progressive Christian, you have shown yourself to be a person who's already done work in the arena of ideas. You've grappled with beliefs you once cherished. Some you ditched, others you renovated. Such grappling evidences a heart that previously had been opened. You could not have engaged in such battles of the mind unless you had already won a war in your heart. To return to the theme of the opening chapters, it required great faith on your part in order to be where you now are.

Our ability to change our minds—and our willingness to admit we were wrong (or at least didn't have the full picture) and to adjust how we see things—plays an enormous role in nurturing our well-being. It's not just that happier people are more open (and by contrast, miserable people are closed off and stuck in their ways), but I do think open people are more likely to find happiness. Don't misunderstand—progressive Christians can be just as stubborn and closed off as anyone. We are not immune from getting off track. But we at least have in our history moments when our hearts opened just enough, when we turned toward the light just enough, so that the seeds of transformation could take root.

It's like how moms who give birth to fraternal twins become more likely to have twins again. When you've taken yourself through the process of being open to change, then actually undergo said change, you're laying down bread crumbs so that you're more likely to follow such a trail again. Openness begets more openness. This bodes well for you, dear reader. Your track record of openness indicates to me a formula for enjoying a life of flourishing. You would do well to occasionally pause and give thanks for the roads you've traveled. How amazing that somewhere along the way, you picked up the value of trust and openness, and how beautiful that you courageously put them into practice. Such bravery deserves applause!

By now we've all heard the words of Paul Tillich (popularized by Anne Lamott) that the opposite of faith is not doubt; it's certainty. Staying open guards us from rushing to certainty. Wisdom involves delaying gratification, where we might need to sit with the unknowing for a while. Embrace the virtue of doubt, for it is in questioning our beliefs that we inoculate ourselves from childish credulity. In the words of Lloyd Geering,

> Doubt is not the enemy of faith, but of false beliefs. Indeed, our entire catalogue of assumptions and beliefs should be continually subjected to critical examination, and those found to be false or inadequate should be replaced by those we find convincing within our cultural context. Yet expressing or even entertaining doubt sometimes takes so much courage that we may say it takes real faith to doubt.[1]

May you commit to remaining as open as possible, trusting that life really is not about getting it right or arriving at some perfect state. After all, the journey, far more than the destination, is what matters. To get the most meaning and enjoyment out of life, may we know love, give love, and receive love all along the way.

TRANSCEND AND INCLUDE

Many people burned by the church or wounded by their previous faith communities end up defining themselves by what they are not: ex-Christian, ex-fundamentalist, ex-evangelical, etc. No doubt I

---

1 Lloyd Geering, *Reimagining God: The Faith Journey of a Modern Heretic* (Salem, OR: Polebridge, 2014), chapter 2.

understand this choice and empathize with a similar urge. However, I fear that anytime we define ourselves by what we are against, we risk getting stuck in the swamps of bitterness and cynicism, which result in a closed-off posture—the opposite of fertile ground for a flourishing life.

Years ago, I heard the phrase *transcend and include* at an event with author and speaker Rob Bell. I don't exaggerate when I say, more than anything else—perhaps other than rewatching sitcoms at night in bed with Kate, such as *The Office*, *Parks & Rec*, and *How I Met Your Mother*—this concept has kept me sane these past several years. This simple yet profound motto creates an expansive horizon in which we can embrace the roads that got us here, leverage whatever insights and lessons we learned along the way, and proceed down a new and more open path in an alternate direction. Stretching both behind and ahead on the timeline of our lives, transcend and include redeems our pasts while paving a more holistic way forward.

To *transcend* suggests we've evolved beyond a given belief or practice. It means we're no longer subjecting ourselves to them as capital-T Truth. It means we have outgrown their usefulness. Simply, we're not where we used to be.

To *include* implies a conscious choice to bring with us that which still contains value from whatever we've transcended. It means the baby is still good even though the bathwater needs draining. It means we refuse to see our pasts as all bad. It means we respect the nature of transformation and accept that it all belongs.

Transcend and include means we move on *and* bring with. We leave what's heavy and retain what's good. To give you an idea, here's how this concept played out in my life:

Transcend the notion that the most important things to God are the beliefs I hold between my ears, or that a life of faith hinges on possessing correct doctrines with certainty; *include* a posture of openness, trusting that the ground of being is ultimately good and loving.

Transcend the idea that God exists somewhere out there as a separate being who occasionally shows up in the drama of history; *include* every intuition and suggestion that God is love, and in God we all belong as beloved children, never separate from that in which we live and move and have our being.

Transcend thinking Jesus's ultimate concern is that I believe in him as the flesh version of an eternal being sent to change God's mind about me; *include* his vision for the kingdom of God to manifest on Earth through radical hospitality, inclusive love, and restorative justice.

Transcend viewing the Bible as a divinely dictated collection of timeless truths, a perfect account for who God is and what is true; *include* an appreciation and awareness for its capacity to shine the light of inspired wisdom on the nature of what it means to be human.

Transcend thinking of church as a place where I must edit myself in order to fit in, and that I feel obligated to attend because it's the only place I can find God; *include* the amazing magic that happens when I open myself up to others and find true belonging and connection, imagining all the ways a faith community can energize people toward coming more alive.

You can (and should!) transcend many of the ideas, values, and practices you left behind when you exited conservative Christianity. At the same time, give yourself permission to include elements from your past that still have value or make you feel good, or that might contribute toward building the type of life you desire. The rhythm of transcend and include protects us from the closed-offness of bitterness and cynicism, and equips us to embody a more loving and open posture.

WHY I'M KEEPING THE "CHRISTIAN" PART

I've almost walked away from Christianity multiple times. Not for some of the obvious reasons: doubts over Jesus, questions about the Bible, issues with God. No, I've strongly considered dropping the "Christian" part of "progressive Christian" because it's appalling to me what comes to mind for most people these days when they hear the word. Much of what "Christian" implies at the popular level reflects almost the opposite of my values and convictions.

When 80 percent of voters who identified as "white evangelical" vote for a known sexual predator who routinely dehumanizes vulnerable people, I want out.[2]

When the Southern Poverty Law Center publishes an eight-thousand-word article titled "Hate in God's Name" that details all the ways in which Christianity still gets used to animate white supremacy, I want out.[3]

When I watch a movie such as *Boy Erased* and must look away from the screen while Christians demean, abuse, and shame LGBTQ people through reparative therapy, I want out.

At what point have I distanced myself so far from mainstream Christianity that to continue using the label seems misleading and unwise? Like many who've left their conservative roots, I hesitate telling people I'm a Christian (let alone a pastor) not because I'm ashamed of Jesus, but because I'm ashamed of those who claim to believe in Jesus yet seem uninterested in following him. Or, to be more honest, follow him in the ways I have come to value most.

I don't mean to bash Christians. As I've already mentioned, people are the way they are for a damn good reason. Most people I know are genuinely doing their best to live out their convictions

---

2 Exit Polls 2016," CNN.com, November 23, 2016, https://tinyurl.com/y8za29gc.

3 Daryl Johnson, "Hate in God's Name," Southern Poverty Law Center, September 25, 2017, https://tinyurl.com/y4vmzuzu.

with integrity, just like me. It's a both/and situation—I both entirely understand there's good reasons for why a person thinks and acts as they do, and it has created such a terrible representation of what it means to be Christian that I'm not sure I want anything to do with it.

This feeling of "those are not my people" explains why many progressives no longer identify as Christian. Other explanations strike closer to home. Rather than pulling away from the label because we're disillusioned by the voting patterns of born-again Christians, many people endure a pushing away by Christian friends and family over differences in belief and "lifestyle" (used here ironically for my LGBTQ siblings). Regardless of how we got here, many of us ask the same two questions: Am I even a Christian still? If so, do I really want to keep calling myself one?

My spiritual paradigm no longer requires a person to hold specific beliefs, so when people walk away from the faith or stop identifying as Christian, I'm not disturbed by it. In fact, I completely understand. If you're one of the many who simply cannot or do not want to identify as Christian, I hope you feel empowered to do as you see fit.

As for me, though, any time I consider departing from Christianity, I'm haunted by a conviction that welled up inside me one afternoon while I was writing a sermon about the blind man near Jericho in Luke 18:35–42.

Sitting outside the bustling city, the man noticed an unfamiliar energy in the crowd. "What's going on?" he asked anyone who would listen.

"Jesus the Nazarene is passing by," someone muttered. Now, who knows why he thought Jesus might be of some help (maybe that trusty ol' wisdom from within?), but immediately he began shouting for the passing rabbi to pay him attention. The type of shouting that's hard to ignore.

"Hush, man! Don't be so obnoxious," Jesus's disciples said, admonishing the man. "The rabbi has important things to do in Jericho. He doesn't have time to stop. Keep it down!" Unfazed, the man shouted louder, finally catching the ears of Jesus, who stopped dead in his tracks.

At that point, Jesus had options. He could have ignored the man. He could have walked over toward the man. He could have shushed the crowd and had a conversation across the road with the man. What did he do? He "called for the man to be brought to him" (Luke 18:40 CEB). In other words, Jesus turned to the very people who had moments ago blocked, shushed, and altogether restricted this man, and he said, "You go and get him."

Christians have been the source of immense suffering in our society. The margins fill with bodies put there by people who claim allegiance to Christ. Discrimination against LGBTQ people, patriarchal systems weighted to favor men, and policies designed to oppress racial minorities all have been either designed by or supported by those who identify as Christian. My friends, *we* have built the walls blocking, shushing, and restricting people's access to the free-flowing love of God.

Why do I still call myself Christian? Why, after all the ways I've been rejected, ignored, and cast out as a heretic, do I retain the label? Why, after the clothes of conservative Christianity no longer fit, do I still identify as a follower of Jesus? Because I'm haunted by the call to climb down into the ditch, kneel to the one shoved to the margins by the powerful, place their arm around my shoulders, and do my best to show them the way toward unconditional love. I hear Jesus loud and clear saying to me, "You. Hey, you. Yeah, the guy in skinny jeans who helped erect these walls . . . *tear them down immediately.* Go to those you've kept outside and make this right."

I believe if we stay open to it, the flow of unconditional love can save the world, for I know it has saved me. I'm still in the game—

both as a Christian and a pastor—because for better or worse, through Christianity I have found freedom from fear and shame, as well as genuine connection to myself, others, and God. I'm finally learning what it means to be whole, and like many of you, I had to move away from conservative Christianity and toward something more progressive in order to find it.

Yet, becoming a progressive Christian involves no shortage of frustration, confusion, sadness, loneliness, and difficulty. We often feel alone and untethered, and like we constantly have to defend or apologize for ourselves. Many of us traded in a life that mostly made sense for one that floats in waters of uncertainty, questions, paradox, and doubt. Some are lucky to live where they can find new faith communities in which to belong and build authentic relationships, but most go it alone. That only makes the journey harder.

I wrote this book for you, friend, because you're not alone, I promise. You're not crazy and you're not doing it wrong—it's just really, really hard. But I think it is good and holy work, and I've committed to listening for the voice of love to direct me to those places where people have been pushed out and kept out. When I get there, I'll tell them what I tell everyone: "You are a beloved child of the Divine, just as you are. I'm sorry for the way church, religion, and spiritual leaders have made you feel. I'm sorry for the shame they heaped upon you, the guilt they tied you down with, and the ways they tried to control your every move. Come, the great party of love that began long ago still rages, but it's not complete without you."

And if I have to tear down some walls—especially the ones that my own religious communities installed along the way—then so be it.

Care to join me?